COURAGE IN THE FACE OF APERT

Courage in the Face of Apert

VICTORY AGAINST ALL ODDS WHILE LIVING WITH APERT SYNDROME

Shayne Stillar

RenaFaye Productions

Cover Photography by
Rena F. Troy
The photos were taken in Shayne's hometown of Waskish, MN overlooking Upper Red Lake where Shayne has spent many days fishing and exploring.

Copyright © 2021 by Shayne Stillar

All rights reserved. No part of this book may be reproduced in any manner whatsoever without written permission except in the case of brief quotations embodied in critical articles and reviews.

First Printing, 2021

"We would like to thank family and friends for all their generous donations that made this book possible."

~ Shayne and Rena

This book is produced by Rena F. Troy of RenaFaye Productions and Shayne Stillar.

Foreword

It is a distinct pleasure to be invited by Shayne to write a foreword for his book. Indeed, a most personal honor!

I had the privilege of serving as Director and Coordinator of the Cleft Palate and Craniofacial Disorders Clinics and Program in the School of Dentistry at the University of Minnesota from 1977 to the time of my retirement in 2008. Our Clinic's focus and service was to diagnose, evaluate, and recommend treatment for patients with these birth conditions. It was interdisciplinary in nature – patients were seen by as many as 10 different specialists (medical, surgical, dental, speech and hearing, genetic, social, and psychologic) at each visit and followed periodically through their growth and development years.

Recommendations included best practice treatment consistent with the patient's stage of physical and behavioral growth and development. The specific recommendations were discussed with the patient and family. Reports were prepared and sent to the family and, importantly, to the patient's direct care providers in their local community.

I recall, so vividly, Shayne's first visit to our Craniofacial Clinic in the late 1970's with his parents when he was 10 – 11 years of age. Even at that time, I found Shayne to be smart, curious, creative, social, questioning and always wanting to understand what was being done and why. Then, I had the absolute pleasure of observing Shayne's treatment journey and progress through his adolescent and young adult years. During those years, Shayne's parents subscribed to the interdisciplinary treatment planning approach and made thoughtful and informed decisions for him. However, Shayne was always intimately involved with those decisions. I loved that!

What was even more special for me has been the consistent contact and connection with Shayne over his adult years and to the present time. That has been such a valued and cherished association for over 40 years!

Shayne's diagnosis of Apert Syndrome (Acrocephalysyndactyly) is typically characterized by hand and feet webbing and fusing, misshapen cranial bones, progressive immobility of joints and cervical spine, cognitive issues associated with CNS malformations, jaw malformations and dental malocclusion, and eye, ear, and nose concerns. The incidence is rare, occurring in only 1 in about 2 million births.

Shayne has faced life-long issues with expected ear, nose, muscle and joint, eye, and other concerns. Clearly, one might anticipate some possible limitations and significant challenges in physical function and social, emotional, behavioral, and educational achievement. Well, don't apply the words "possible limitations" with Shayne! Those words are simply not in his vocabulary. Shayne graduated from high school, college, and university with a major in radio and TV and went on to more technical training and career in wastewater management. Moreover, Shayne pursued the physical challenges of road cycling and has been a consistent award winner in competitions around the country. He continues to participate in the rigorous training required and success in cycling competitions!

Additionally, over the years, Shayne has shared his life experiences and has challenged and inspired others with Apert Syndrome and similar conditions which are associated with physical and emotional challenges. The diagnosis of Apert simply did not define Shayne Stillar! He was not an Apert patient, but rather a person with a diagnosis of a condition called Apert. And he has demonstrated so convincingly how to rise above the challenges, explore the possibilities, seek out opportunities, and with resolve and fortitude, identify purpose and take charge of his own life journey and destination.

Now, Shayne has prepared this book with the aim and desire to share his experiences, challenges, and opportunities, and to challenge others to reach high and to achieve their potential. To quote Shayne: "I just want to help people!"

I, personally, am so proud of Shayne – his life journey, his achievements and accomplishments, his attitude of gratitude for what he can do despite hurdles along the way. I applaud him and this book! He surely is an inspiration to many including his family and, indeed, to me.

    Karlind T. Moller, Ph.D
    Professor Emeritus
    University of Minnesota
        School of Dentistry and Department of
        Speech-Language-Hearing Sciences
        Former Director and Coordinator–
        Cleft Palate and Craniofacial Program

and emotional challenges. The diagnosis of Apert simply did not define Shayne Stillar! He was not an Apert patient, but rather a person with a diagnosis of a condition called Apert. And he has demonstrated so convincingly how to rise above the challenges, explore the possibilities, seek out opportunities, and with resolve and fortitude, identify purpose and take charge of his own life journey and destination.

Now, Shayne has prepared this book with the aim and desire to share his experiences, challenges, and opportunities, and to challenge others to reach high and to achieve their potential. To quote Shayne: "I just want to help people!"

I, personally, am so proud of Shayne – his life journey, his achievements and accomplishments, his attitude of gratitude for what he can do despite hurdles along the way. I applaud him and this book! He surely is an inspiration to many including his family and, indeed, to me.

    Karlind T. Moller, Ph.D
    Professor Emeritus
    University of Minnesota
     School of Dentistry and Department of
     Speech-Language-Hearing Sciences
     Former Director and Coordinator–
     Cleft Palate and Craniofacial Program

Foreword

We would like to introduce you to someone very special in our lives, our cousin Shayne. Shayne has been more like a brother to we sisters our entire lives. Growing up we watched him live a very normal life with amazing parents who treated him like any other kid. We also witnessed when out in public places, the looks, and the comments and fortunately as he got older Shayne's only desire was to educate those around him about his syndrome. Despite his physical difficulties and the challenges, they presented, Shayne along with his parents would always find a way for him to do anything for which he found a passion.

He is an avid outdoorsman, if he's not fishing or hunting Shayne is riding one of his many bikes and of course, he likes to be with family whenever the opportunity presents itself. His exceptional courage, nobility, strength, and perseverance in how he lives his life distinguish Shayne. Heroes are defined in many different ways. Heroes are people we look up to, heroes are people who overcome great odds, and heroes go above and beyond despite the odds against them. This is the story of our favorite hero, and we are willing to put him up against any hero that has ever come before him.

- Stephanie Lundin Kemp and
Wendy Lundin Kingbay

Foreword

I first met Shayne when I was 16 years-old in International Falls, Minnesota. I'm now 47. I was visiting my grandparents who lived in 'The Falls'. There was the annual local bike race that weekend called 'To Hill and Back' that I was going to participate in. Bike racing was a huge part of my life, and I was eager to show off in front of my grandparents.

The night before the race my grandfather said he wanted me to meet 'an amazing young man'. He told me a little about Shayne's background with Apert Syndrome and how Shayne had endured countless surgeries. Moreover, he told me that Shayne was crazy about bike racing, fishing, and hunting – all things I love.

The next morning racers arrived at the start and my grandfather introduced me to Shayne and his father. We chatted a million miles an hour which helped with the nerves of the race to come. The race starts and quickly there is separation with the faster riders going off the front of a large group. Shayne was in the front pack.

I could tell lots of stories in the many years that have passed since we first met - how he remembers everyone's birthdays, how he keeps tabs on everyone he cares about and sends messages, notes, or calls to check in, how he is often the glue of relationships, how he inspires others within the Apert community, cycling community and more. They all conclude the same – Shayne is in the front pack of whatever the story is about.

    I've had the honor of calling Shayne my friend since I was 16. After a few years of our friendship Shayne would say 'you are like family to me' which was certainly a reciprocated feeling. When his mother died, I attended the funeral along with my dad. After the service Shayne, both our fathers and I were chatting. I'm not great at family trees, but somebody from my dad's family married somebody from Shayne's dad's family and Shayne quickly ran the lineage in his head to figure out we are in fact cousins. "I knew it!" he exclaimed.

    Shayne is definitely in the front pack of whatever he does but this is especially true with family and friends (and friends are family to Shayne). I broke my leg and pelvis in 2008 and Shayne was on the phone guiding me through how to deal with the physical pain and disappointment that my racing season would be over before it started. Shayne is a definitive expert on the subject. Shayne broke his hip at a bike race once, but handled it with grace, humility, optimism, and hope; essentially writing the true book of rehabilitation. Shayne gave me no choice but to chin up and get back in the front pack.

    Life has flown by. It seems like yesterday I was 16 and meeting Shayne. Today I have a wife and 2 kids, a great career and a happy life. We are a product of our environments, most notably our friends and family. Anyone who has met Shayne is a better person for it. He'll inspire you to be in the front pack and will give you a push, if need be, to keep you there.

- Jeremy Sartain

Contents

Foreword	vii
Foreword	xi
Foreword	xiii
Dedication	xvii
Introduction	xix

1	An Uncertain Beginning	1
2	My Chewbacca Socks	7
3	Life Bigger Than Survival	18
4	Hunting and Racing	34
5	Broadsided But Not Beaten	45
6	Most Tenacious	56
7	Old Goats	63
8	Getting to Know My Body Better	69
9	Bike Champion	78
10	As Long as I Can Fish	85
11	An Elite Cyclist	94
12	Duathlon? Why Not!	100

13	Running the Race	108
14	Tough Changes	114
15	Why Not Triathlons?	122
16	A New Nemesis	130
17	A Golden Mistake	139
18	Minnesota Determination	147
19	My Dad	156
20	What's Next	161
21	Epilogue	166

This book is dedicated to my parents,
Patrick and Jacque Stillar who gave me
life and never gave up on me, nor did they
ever let me give up on myself.

This is also dedicated to the doctors and
medical staff over the years who worked
hard to offer me a chance at reaching my
goals and dreams ~
and to my family, friends, and fellow
teammates along the way,
whose love and
encouragement is priceless to me.

~ Shayne

Introduction

In the first part of this book, you will find out about who I am and where I came from. It will explain the difficulties I have encountered with my start in life and living with Apert Syndrome.

My struggles to live a normal life, as most people know it, have been a challenge that I fight every day. You will come with me as I look at my life as an adult, my education, employment, and achievements. Every little step for me has been an uphill battle.

Thanks to my wonderful parents, Patrick and Jacque Stillar. Because of them, I was able to face this life with the best of what they had instilled in me and what they taught me. Also, I thank them for not changing their passion for the outdoors just because they had a special needs son. They found a way to introduce me to their love for the outdoors and in turn it has helped me on my journey through life. I include my hunting and fishing stories in this book as well as my love for competition and personal achievement.

I hope you enjoy the rest of the book. If you take anything away from my life story, I hope and pray that it is the reality that 'anything is possible as long as you have the dream to do something'.

~ Shayne Stillar

1

An Uncertain Beginning

On the second day of summer in 1966, I came into this world. I was born to Patrick and Jacque Stillar of International Falls, Minnesota, on Wednesday, June 22, 1966. I began my journey with obstacles in my path, and never a day went by that I wasn't reminded that my life was a constant uphill battle. My mother almost died giving birth to me. I was breech in my mother's womb. Instead of the doctors doing a C-Section to get me out, the doctor forced my mother to have me normally. After I was born, the doctors informed my parents that their son was born with a rare syndrome known as Apert Syndrome.

I was born with "mitt" hands; my fingers were webbed together. My toes were fused and webbed. My head was not formed right. I was also born with hydrocephalus, which means that I had fluid pressure on my brain.

In October of that year, my parents had to take me to the University of Minnesota Hospital, where the doctors opened my head so they could relieve the pressure on my brain. Also, when I was born, the doctors had told my parents that I probably would not live long, and if I did, I would never walk.

In addition to everything, I was born with a cleft palate, which made it difficult for me to start speaking. In April of 1969, my parents took me back to the University of Minnesota Hospital, where the doctors went in and repaired my cleft palate. Even though I was sent to a speech therapist, my voice sounded different to my peers and the public. Because of that, I was a quiet kid. I knew I sounded different than other people. I didn't often speak so I wouldn't get teased.

I had to learn to do things with my hands that were simple for most children, but my fingers were fused, making the simplest thing difficult. My thumb wasn't fused, but it was short and fat. I went back to the U of M Hospital in September of 1969 to have surgery to separate the fingers on my right hand. They divided my small finger from the one next to it. Then they separated the middle two of the five fingers, but they left my pointer and my middle finger together. They did a skin graph from my upper right leg to use for webbing between my thumb and my pointer finger. A few weeks later, they changed my cast and removed the stitches. Then in March of 1970, they repeated the same procedure on my left hand.

Now, I do not know if I was in the room when the doctors told my parents that I would probably never walk. I was too young to remember. But my dad informed me that it was on my 2nd Christmas in 1967; we were at my mom's parent's place on Island Lake in Northome, MN when I took my first steps. I walked from my mother's arms to him. He told me that they all cheered and were overwhelmed with joy. I had proved the doctors to be wrong. These were not the last people I proved wrong in my life. I was to face and overcome many challenges as I moved forward.

Living with Apert Syndrome has not been easy by any means. First, I do not remember too much about my childhood because of the trauma I went through, though I knew that it was tough and that every day was a challenge.

Being a special needs child was hard, but I did not know that I was 'not normal.' My parents made sure of that. They raised me as a normal child. I was taught to respect my elders and to follow their rules. If I didn't, I was disciplined.

I had very few friends. I had to play alone most of the time. My parents and I lived about 4 miles from International Falls in the country. The Pullar family lived a short distance from us. I became friends with their youngest son. He let me sit with him on the school bus even though he was a few years older than me. I would have my mother call his parents to see if he would come and play with me, and usually, he did. He would also come and watch me as a babysitter. All his brothers and sisters babysat me, except for the one sister who was a year younger than I.

It didn't take long for Dad and Mom to introduce me to the great outdoors. They told me that they had me out in a boat when I was only two weeks old. I am sure they had me with them in the car when my parents would go out grouse hunting or deer hunting in the fall of the year. I was raised loving the outdoors. I am glad that my parents hunted and fished, though they only hunted deer and grouse.

Dad gave me a fishing pole when I was old enough to hold one. My mom's dad, Grandpa Max Unger, would get frustrated because I would have my line in and out of the water constantly, and I usually out fished him. My parents would buy me toy guns, too. They also taught me gun safety. When I was old enough, my dad bought me a BB gun. I would go outside often and target practice with empty pop cans.

When Dad would need to get gravel for something, I would go with him, and he'd get me a can of pop. The gravel pit had a deep-water area. I would throw the pop can in and see how many shots it took me to sink it.

When I was in my mid-teens, my parents bought me an air rifle. I would have the job of keeping the squirrels away from the bird feeder in the winter months.

I was taught by my parents to follow orders and to respect my elders. I knew what was coming if I didn't. I wish more parents would discipline their children as my parents disciplined me. Maybe if they did, more kids would respect their parents, grandparents, and the authorities. It is something that is missing today - respect.

Studying in school was difficult. I know I should have done better. A problem I encountered was that no matter how hard I studied for a test, my mind would freeze up on me when it came time to take it. The other problem I encountered was – I did not like being inside and studying. I wanted to be outside playing with my trucks in the sandpile, or in my treehouse, or hunting or fishing, or anything - but studying.

I can look back and see the things I wished I worked harder at or things I wished I could have changed, but now I realize that I traveled the road the good Lord put me in this world to follow. It was a hard road, but a good one.

My mom and dad - Jacque and Patrick Stillar and me

*" I had proved the doctors to be wrong.
These were not the last people I proved wrong in my life.
I was to face and overcome many challenges
as I moved forward."*

2

My Chewbacca Socks

My formal education began in 1971. I entered preschool in International Falls. Then in the school year of 1972 – 1973, I went to kindergarten. I'm not sure, but I think I started kindergarten at International Falls Elementary but shortly transferred to the kindergarten at Alexander Bauer School in Int'l Falls.

After I completed kindergarten, my parents had a huge fight on their hands because the International Falls school administration tried to force my parents to put me into special education classes only. Since I was born with Apert Syndrome, the school administration did not think I could handle a regular class setting. My parents, along with the help of my speech therapist, Mr. Roger Geddes, fought to get me into 'normal' school. My parents were able to persuade the school administration that I would be able to handle a regular classroom.

I went to Forestland Elementary in the Falls for the first and second grades. For some reason, after going through the first grade, I could not advance to second grade. But after my second year of the first grade, I was able to move on.

As a second grader, I started to wonder what it would be like to be able to be in the front of the line at recess. My stubbornness never allowed me to make it happen. One spring day, I told myself that I was going to do it. But I ended up getting scared and nervous and got into my usual place at the back of the line. This day was etched into my memory, and I think about it when I now face obstacles that I want to overcome. I don't want to be that scared second-grader anymore. My curiosity drove my independence from that day on.

In third grade, I had Mrs. Terri Kjellgren for a teacher. In the fourth grade, I had my first male teacher, Mr. Tom Manka. He was a particularly good teacher. I didn't get into deep trouble, but once I lied about my test score for a particular test because I knew I did not do well on it. Luckily, I just got a good scolding for it.

Mr. Manka was good to me in other ways. International Falls had three elementary schools in town. Each spring, the three schools had a track and field meet between them. Even though I had severe disabilities, I tried my hardest to qualify for an event. I was going to sign up for one of the hurdle events. Mr. Manka was the Alexander Baker 4th grade coach. He saw me lining up and told me, "No, Shayne, I don't want you to try this one." I was so frustrated because my parents taught me never to give up or say that I couldn't do something without trying it first. Later that day, when the class was lining up at the door to go somewhere, Mr. Manka announced to the class that I would be his manager for the next track meet. I got to go to the track meet, but as a student manager and his assistant. He made me feel that I was an important part of the team.

My fifth grade went on, but that is where I (and a few others) fell behind in doing specific reading levels for that grade. My sixth grade was also good, and so was my sixth-grade teacher.

There were many struggles during my school years. I think it was in the third grade when I was introduced to bullying. My classmates began to tease and pick on me, especially at recess, especially if they were picking teams. I was always the last to be picked.

I did have a good friend at Alexander Baker Elementary whose name was Mikol Nelson. I had other friends, but they went to Falls Elementary. I knew why I was teased and picked on. I wore thick heavy glasses when I was young, plus I had to wear special shoes because my toes were webbed and fused together. I had other severe disabilities that, at the time, I did not realize that I had.

I was stared at by other children and adults when I was out in public through the first 14 years of my life, especially when I was school age. Besides the stares, there were the quiet comments made among themselves about my appearance. It frustrated me when other children were doing it, especially when their parents were with them. It did get better after my mid-face surgeries. But even today, more so when I am in South Texas, I get those same stares and whispers. I have had two medical eye doctors who think that I am mentally handicapped because they see my disabilities and assume the rest. I also think two eye technicians thought the same as these doctors did.

When I was going to school from 1st through 12th grade, I was seldom invited to my classmate's birthday parties. Even in the area where I lived, I wasn't asked, except for my best friend, who only lived two driveways away from ours. Then a few times to our neighbor's daughters' birthdays. But that was it. Whenever grade school dances started, I never attended because I figured that I would be teased or ignored if I did go, so I never went.

One of my strengths, when I was a child was that I was very stubborn. I hated asking for help. Being stubborn was good in that I saw myself as normal. When someone would tell me that I couldn't do something, it just made me more determined to prove them wrong. Sometimes it meant coming up with my own way to do the task. My parents treated me as a normal kid at home, so I thought it would be the same way at school, but that was not the case.

There were quite a few days in a school year that I would fake being sick, so I did not have to go. I knew that it would put me behind in school, but I just couldn't face the cruelty of the kids at those times. Not all the kids were nice to me. It wasn't until 11th grade that my peers accepted me.

In 1979 I had my first eye surgery. My eye doctor in Duluth found a white spot on my right eye and did not know what it was. He sent me to the University of Minnesota Hospital to get it checked out. The eye doctor there decided they needed to do a biopsy, which meant surgery. They set a date for surgery. My parents and I drove down the night before to the University to get me checked in. I was so nervous that night; I could not get any sleep.

They almost canceled my surgery. Dad had made me a promise that if I went through the surgery, he would buy me a Star Wars X-Wing Fighter. Luckily, the doctors decided to do the biopsy. On the way up to Hibbing to my grandparent's place, Dad stopped and kept his word and bought me the fighter. The verdict came back on my biopsy, and we found out it was just some degenerated cells that had gathered there; this created a unique situation. The right eye with the spot was near-sighted, and my left eye was far-sighted. They worked together to help me see.

After sixth grade, I advanced to the seventh grade at Backus Middle School. That is when life became more challenging. Even though I had more friends, I was subjected to more teasing. It was also in the 7th grade where I had the first part of my mid-face reconstruction surgery.

It was at the beginning of my 7th grade at school, my first year at Middle School. I had new classmates to get used to and being a young man with severe disabilities was not easy. I was teased and picked on by the other students.

When I was 14 years old, my parents told me that we would be going on a weeklong vacation. They said that we were going to Thunder Bay, Ontario, and then make our way down back into the United States along the North Shore of Lake Superior. Then they told me that we would end the vacation at the University of Minnesota Hospital Cleft Palette & Cranial Clinic.

The trip was great. When we got back into the U.S., my parents took me to a Target store. The movie "Star Wars" had been out, so they bought me some socks that had Star Wars characters on them. I chose Chewbacca socks.

The day after we arrived in Minneapolis, we headed to my appointment at the clinic. My parents had to make a very tough decision, hopefully changing my life for the better. I was going to be only the second person in Minnesota to ever have mid-face reconstruction surgery. It was going to be risky because my brain was going to be exposed for an extended time. The surgery was divided into two parts, and both times, they would have to expose my brain. Part two of the surgery was to take place six months later.

I made it to my first appointment. That is when we met Dr. Karlind Moller and his staff. Dr. Moller greeted us and started going over what they were going to have to do. They told us that first, they were going to take impressions of my mouth. That is when I lost it and started crying. I had already had a few impressions taken from the dentists before, and I had difficulty with them. Dr. Moller and two of his nurses asked me to go to another room. When we got to the other room, the nurses noticed my Chewbacca socks. They went crazy over them. Dr. Moller had told the nurses that I was afraid, and they did what they could to calm me down. They told me not to worry. They did things differently there. It was better than what I experienced before. They started the process of setting up my appointment to have the surgery done.

The day came for me to go back to the University of Minnesota Hospital for my surgery. They checked me into one of their children's wards. I had a couple of roommates. Both of them had leukemia.

Dr. Shelley Chou did the first part of my surgery. Just before they took me into the operating room, they stopped and shaved my head. During the surgery, they took out pieces of my hip bones to put around my eyes to create my brow. They did this to make my eyes look more normal. They also opened my skull from ear to ear. They did the work they had to do to make my skull better shaped to fit my brain. They closed my skull cap with over 100 steel wire stitches.

The first part of the surgery went well, but I had to stay in the hospital for quite a while. I was finally able to go home and eventually get back to school.

My return to 7th grade became extremely difficult. My classmates did not understand why I had to wear a surgical cap on my head. They did not know that I still had 100 stitches from ear to ear. The kids would always try and take the cap off my head, throw it, and then laugh at me because I was still bald from the surgery. Things got a little better after I was able to get my stitches out, and my hair started to grow back, but I still got teased occasionally.

Starting a new school and grade with new classmates plus going through the first part of major reconstruction surgery that could have ended with me dying was tough. But I had family and friends for support.

I was able to finish the seventh grade, and summer came. Now I had to go back for the second part of the surgery. This part would be rougher because I would have to have my eyes bandaged and stitched shut for three days. I would also have my jaw wired shut for six weeks and have a tracheotomy in my throat for a week. I was not going to be able to talk or eat normally.

We got to the hospital and got checked in, but I lost it again when they took me to my room. I started crying. I was so scared. They had me admitted me in the adult area of the hospital and had a room to myself. I knew I was going to miss having roommates. It took a while, but I eventually calmed down and accepted the fact that I had to be there.

That evening, Dr. Alan Shons came in to meet me. He was going to be doing the surgery. They began to prep me to get the labs done because they would do the surgery in the morning. I told him that I already had all these tests done before, but he did them again anyway on the spot.

The next morning, they wheeled me to surgery and shaved my head again. They showed me the recovery room and the ICU the day before, so I would know where I would be when I woke up since my eyes would be stitched shut and I would not be able to see, nor would I be able to talk. It helped calm my anxiety a bit.

The time right after surgery, I do not remember. I did need to learn how to write with my eyes closed so I could tell the nurses when I was feeling nauseous, and they needed to maintain my trach. I was in ICU for three days, and they moved me back to my room. There they unbandaged my eyes and took the stitches out. I could now see but still could not talk. They took my trach out a week later.

Things got better when they took the trach out because I could finally talk, well, sort of. My jaw was still wired shut. The food was terrible because everything had to be liquefied to get it into my mouth.

I was in the hospital for three weeks, and then they let me go home. They told my parents and me that if I ever broke the plastic plate that was put into my forehead, I would probably die because it would hit my brain.

Shortly after I got home, my best friend Brad Larson came back from Arizona. He came back excited about a new sport he found down there—something for both of us to get involved with. The sport was Bicycle Motocross. I did not know it at the time, but this was the beginning of a life-long passion. It would be something that would change my life.

Living with Apert had affected me emotionally in many ways because I had gone through so many surgeries when I was young. I remember little of my childhood because I blocked some of the most painful memories out.

I was in my early teens before I was able to stay home alone at night. I had it in my head that when my parents would leave me alone and go out for the evening, it meant I would get an operation the following day. I feared the pins and needles that I would have to endure in preparation for each surgery. I finally got over that fear and realized that my parents going out for an evening didn't mean I would have surgery the next day. It took quite a while for that to sink into my head. The fear was so intense. There are no words to describe what I went through with my two mid-face operations. My parents were honest with me and had told me before each surgery that I could die from going through the procedure. With that knowledge, I was forced to become an adult at the tender age of 14.

These surgeries also affected my peers and how they treated me, especially in high school. Soon after I got done with my last mid-face surgery, I sat myself down and thought, "I do not know what my future will be like with this syndrome, so I'm not going to smoke, drink or do drugs." I knew my peers were having parties and consuming alcohol. I refused to participate because living with Apert was hard enough; I didn't want to complicate things. I made that promise to myself. My parents never smoked or used drugs. They did, however, have a few drinks now and then, but they did it in moderation. To this day, I have not broken that promise to myself.

It was rough being an only child, and since both my parents worked, it was rough for them to give me the attention and the medical attention that I needed. I had always wanted to have an older sister. I desired that most when I went through my last major mid-face surgery. I think it would have made it easier for my parents. My Aunt Deb and Uncle Curt had two daughters who are close to me. Even though they are cousins about 4 and 6 years younger than me, they have always felt like sisters.

My best friend Brad Larson is like a brother to me. Either I was at his house, or he was at mine through the years. But I think having a sibling would have been wonderful. Not sure why, but having an older sister was always something I always longed for. I am a competitive person, so I don't think having a brother would have been a good idea.

My first 2 wheel bicycle

Me and Dad

Mom and I

3

Life Bigger Than Survival

Being born with Apert did not allow me to go out for sports when I was young. I had three and a half fingers on each hand, plus my legs and feet are not normal either. I'm rather glad that Apert kept me out of sports until I was 14 because if I had a bad game, I know I would have had a coach, teammates, and other parents upset with me.

In the summer of 1980, I just finished the most difficult operations that I had gone through in my life. I felt good about it. Now, my appearance was a lot more acceptable to the public, though my peers still teased me.

When I got home from the hospital, and Brad had informed me about bicycle motocross. I was so excited. Because of my deformities due to the Apert, my structure, and disability in my hands, performing most sports was challenging for me. With bicycle motocross, I felt it was something I could do despite my disabilities. I finally found a sport where if I had a bad day, the only person I would be letting down is myself.

I began reading about bicycle motocross in the Junior National Geographic magazine that my parents had gotten me. I only had a single-speed bike, but I put a banana seat on it, then motocross handlebars. I called it "General Lee" because I loved the show "The Dukes of Hazard."

It was also in 1980 when I bought my first shotgun. I saw a 410-shotgun in a Christmas catalog. It cost $99. I had just received just over $100 in my get-well cards from my hospital stay, so I asked my parents if I could use that to get the gun. They told me it was a good idea and they ordered it for me.

I took firearm safety training that fall. I passed with flying colors. I had 4 out of the five shots in my shooting test hit the bull's eye using a 22-caliber rifle. This was also the year I started buying my own fishing poles and tackle.

In the spring of 1980 or 1981, the neighborhood kids on my bus told me they were heading out and doing some sucker fishing. Suckers are a rough kind of bottom-feeding fish. I went with them and had a great time. From then on, it was a tradition to go sucker fishing every spring in the creeks.

We lived about four miles out of town. My parents had about three and a half acres of land, and most of it was woods. My dad made trails that ran through the woods in several directions. Just north of their land was a huge wild field and just north of that was a good-sized swamp. Some of the swamp was privately owned, but the land was never posted. Our land and this swamp are where I spent a lot of time when I was young.

Dad would tell me stories of when he was young, that he had a trapline. He trapped mink, muskrat, weasel, and other fur-bearing animals. I started trapping animals that I could eat like rabbits. I also trapped weasels and squirrels.

Then when I was able to drive, I started going after mink, muskrat, fisher, pine martins, and fox. I had about 50 – 70 miles to drive to check all my traps, plus a mile walk behind our house for my traps there.

I caught several fishers and pine martins. I had one red fox that my parents had the hide tanned for me. It is hanging in my training room. I have fond memories of my trapping days. I love getting out and spending time in the woods.

One day in 1982, my friend Brad called me and told me that Woolco, the department store in the local mall, had two motocross bikes for sale. One with mag wheels and one with spokes. The next time my parents took me to the store, I checked them out. I fell in love with the one with mag wheels. I started saving my money. Plus, I started bugging my parents about the bike.

June 22, 1982, my parents had a small birthday party for me. My grandparents on my mom's side came, plus my aunt, uncle, and cousins from Hibbing. My friend Brad was there too. I had opened all my gifts, so I thought, and had eaten when my dad came and got me. I was in my bedroom with Brad and my cousins. Dad told me that my uncle and grandpa wanted to see me. We all come out of the bedroom. I was in the lead. That is when I saw the chrome motocross bicycle with the mag wheels sitting in our living room. I was shocked but thrilled. I immediately took it for a spin in the driveway. Dad didn't let me ride too long because it was raining outside.

Later that summer, my parents had a yard party. The staff and the truckers who worked for the truck lines just down the road from us were there. One trucker's wife told me that they had a BMX track in the city of Moose Lake, where they lived. We set a date to where we could visit Moose Lake.

The day came for our trip to Moose Lake for a visit. Later that day, we went to the BMX track. I had brought my bike with me. I registered to take part in the day's race and hit the track. When I got to the top of the track and looked down, I got scared big time. The ramp was about 10 feet tall, and it had a steep angle to it. I finally got the nerve to make my first practice run. Then I tried two more times. Each time I was scared. I told my parents that I was going to pull out of the race. I told them that I wasn't ready. We did stay and watch some of the races that day. That was the height of my racing for 1982.

In 1983, Brad and I discovered that they had just opened a BMX track in Virginia, MN, which is a lot closer to home than Moose Lake. On one of our family trips to Duluth, my dad stopped at the track in Virginia. I got out and went to the starting hill. This one wasn't as high as the one in Moose Lake, plus it was not as steep. We made plans and told Brad's mother that I wanted to try this track and asked if Brad could come with me.

This time I registered for the race and had no problems doing the quarter-mile course. I did not make it out of the qualifying heats, but I think Brad did. Most importantly, we both had fun. My biggest problem was that I did not have a quick speed. I was getting going just when the race was over.

I raced a few more times in 1983 and 1984. I did race in Bagley with Brad, but I never made it to the main event again. I retired from motocross racing in 1985. I decided to go into road cycling. I found that suited me better.

When I was racing motocross - 1983 in Virginia, MN

*

Eighth grade went better, basically since I didn't have any surgeries that year. I was finally done for a while. Still, some of my classmates were not all that nice to me. I did okay, grade-wise, but I was a C-average student. I did make the B Honor Roll a few times, but I can't remember what grades they were.

In the ninth grade, I was still being picked on by my peers in physical education class. Mr. Gjertson, my physical education teacher, was exceptional and treated me like a normal kid, unlike my physical education teachers in elementary school. When it came to the President's Physical Fitness Test, my physical education teachers in the 7th through 9th grades allowed me to try my best. When it came time to see how many pull-ups I could do, they allowed me to try doing them my way. Because my fingers are short and do not bend, I had to turn my hand around and use my wrists to hook the bar. This worked, and I was able to do the pull-ups. My 1st through 6th-grade physical education teacher would not allow me to try even though I told him that I thought I could do it. I wanted to do it my way in his class, but he would not allow it, which made me angry because he wouldn't let me try.

Mr. Gjertson in high school also helped in other ways. One day we played basketball, and I was dribbling the ball, but I was double dribbling, but I didn't know it. The opposing team started to complain to Mr. Gjertson about my dribbling. He said to the guys, "Don't you know what that is?" They said, "No." He told them that it was a 'Shayne Dribble' and they quit complaining.

In the ninth grade, I broke the first bone in my body. The morning after our first snowfall in International Falls, I was at my locker and was heading to my first-hour class, which was art class. I had just started going around a corner in the hallway, and I slipped on the melted snow and fell. I landed on my elbow. I got up and proceeded to my class. When I got to the class, I knew something was not right. My right elbow was sore, and I was in pain. The pain was still manageable, so I was not in tears. My classmates did not believe me when I told them that I thought I broke my elbow. They told me that if it were broken, that I would be crying. I explained that I had a higher pain tolerance than most kids because of my past surgeries. I told my teacher that I better go down to Mr. Bilben, the principal's office.

When I got down to the office, I told them that I just broke my arm and needed to call my parents to come and get me to go to the doctor. Mr. Bilben called my mother and said that I was in the office because I thought I had broken my elbow. He told my mother that he didn't believe that it was broken. My mother came and got me and took me to our family doctor. I was right. After they took x-rays, it showed that I had fractured my right elbow. They sent me the next day to Hibbing to see a specialist. Luckily, the fracture was clean and stayed in place, so no surgery was required.

The summer after ninth grade, I reached a huge achievement. Since I was held back in the first grade, I was old enough to take my driver's education and then take the test right away. I passed both the written part and the driving part on my first try.

I purchased my first nice rod and reel for fishing the year I was able to drive. This guy I knew that worked at the bike shop in town came over to me one night when I was fishing. He showed me what he was using and told me that I should get the same type of rod. I took his advice, and now I always make sure my walleye rod is a light-medium action.

It was nicer now that I could drive because our parents would let me take our 14-foot Lund fishing boat alone to the lakes. I would fish for walleye, bass, northern, sunfish, or crappie.

My love of hunting and fishing is about the same, but hunting is easier; all I need is my car or a 4-wheeler and my gun or a crossbow. Also, hunting is in the fall when it is cooler. I also like to take my mountain bike to go grouse hunting because I go on trails that are closed to motorized vehicles.

For the most part, 10th grade was uneventful, though my classmates started being nice to me. I finally felt that I was part of the class. That was because I had decided to play goalie for soccer, broomball, and floor hockey. I had good defense techniques.

In the spring of my 10th grade, I was picking my classes for the 11th grade. I saw a class called "Survival" and knew many of my friends were planning on taking it. I wanted to take it, too, because I was raised hunting and fishing. I knew this class was going to be a good fit for me. There was one requirement that I needed to have before I could take that class, and that was I had to know how to swim. I had never learned how to swim. I was lucky because Mr. Tom Gerardy was the course instructor for the survival class. He was also my 8th-grade geography teacher. I approached him one day and let him know that I'd like to take the survival class the following year, but I had a problem, and it was that I did not know how to swim. He said that he could help me out.

Mr. Gerardy asked me if I had study hall the first hour that coming year, which I did. He told me to tell the study hall monitor that I was going to see him that hour. We met at the pool. Mr. Gerardy taught me to swim. I was happy because now I was able to sign up for the survival class for my junior year.

My junior year was a lot more eventful for me in more ways than one. It started great the first day. I told my first hour Study Hall Monitor that I'd be going to the pool to meet Mr. Gerardy for the rest of the quarter or until he told me that I was good enough. The hall monitor remembered and told me that it would be no problem.

My first swim lesson went great. I got the breaststroke down quickly. The fly or freestyle was more challenging due to the way my arms and shoulders were shaped. That was the same with the backstroke, but I was able to do that okay.

My junior year was going well until one morning in my 4th-hour history class. The teacher was Rodney Max. Things were fine when I walked into class, but they changed quickly. Mr. Max started reading off the Falls Senior Highschool Hit List of the people who came late to school. Well, he read off my name. Then he said, "Well, we know now who shot a hole in our window." Yes, there was a hole in one of the windows, but I did not do it. I just said "Okay" and did not try to defend myself. After class, I went into the office and found out that my study hall monitor had forgotten that I was taking swimming lessons with Mr. Gerardy and had reported me absent. I thought I had everything cleared up, but the next day I found out I was wrong.

Mr. Max brought up that he thought it was me that broke the window, and I believe he started adding more to his story. Again, I just sat at my desk and did not say a word, nor did I defend myself. I was taught not to talk back to my teachers. This situation continued to go on daily at the start of history class. Finally, I told my parents that I had enough, and if they got a call from the office, they would know why. The Friday before the opening of firearm deer hunting season, I walked into my history class and sat down. Mr. Max started in on me again. I finally opened my mouth and started to defend myself. The whole room got silent. The rest of the day, when Mr. Max saw me in the hallway, he tried to pin something on me, but I was ready to "give it right back" to him.

The following Monday was parent-teacher conferences. My mother went in to see my teachers. They all told her that I was a good student. But when she went to see Mr. Max, my history teacher, he asked her if she and my dad knew that he had been picking on me. My mother told him that "yes, she knew all about it." He then asked her if she and my dad wanted him to stop. My mother told him "no that he did not have to stop picking on me." But she warned him that I was now out of their hands and that I had every right to defend myself.

From that day on, Mr. Max and I became friends, and he began to treat me with respect. I'm pretty sure the reason why he started picking on me like he did; was he wanted to give me a push. He knew I was smarter than the rest of my classmates thought I was. He also knew that I was afraid to ask or answer questions in school. I was scared of being wrong and being teased by my classmates. I look back now, and I'm thankful he did what he did.

I also took woodworking in my junior year. I had Mr. Jon Knutson as a teacher. He was a great teacher to me. My big wood project was making a gun cabinet in one of the Christmas or Fall catalogs. Mr. Knutson always made sure that if there was any possible danger, that something might happen, he was there to help me do what needed to be done.

The other woodworking instructor in school, Mr. Villalta, was great, too. He treated me normally but was also willing to help me if I felt scared about using a machine. Others treated me normally also, but I don't recall their names. My physical education teacher, Mr. Reed, was also very respectful to me and was not afraid to do a slap shot when I was in the net for floor hockey.

The summer after my junior year, my parents and I started thinking about college. My parent's friend told my parents that I could probably get help through the State Department of Rehabilitation. We went in and met with the guy in charge. He said that I should go and take a test. The test went on until it came time to see what I could do with my hands. The first test was to put washers on little bolts. The instructor looked at me and said, "Mr. Stillar, you do not have to do this test." I asked her, "Why?" She said, "because of the deformities in both of my hands." I told her, "Listen, yes, I do have deformities and disabilities in my hands. The others who have taken this test will probably be faster than I, but what we do not know yet is what I can do. So just say 'go' and start your watch and let's see what I can do." Well, the results came back. They told me that the only job I could do was to become a park ranger. So, I had to take algebra in my senior year of high school to meet the requirements.

My senior year of high school went very well, and I made it through all my classes okay, though I changed my college plans. Our senior class had taken a field trip to Rainy River Community College, and while on tour, they took us by a classroom. They said that this was their mass communication department for radio and TV broadcasting. Right then is when I knew what I wanted to do. When I got home, I told my parents that I would become a television cameraman for the news.

In my senior year, one of my high school counselors tried to discourage me from going to college. He told me that I was not really "college material." But just like the kids that bullied me when I was young. I shrugged it off, and I just kept believing in myself.

I told my Department of Rehabilitation Counselor what I was going to do. I walked into my high school graduation and received my diploma. For someone who was thought not to walk, talk, or even live until I was ten years old. I had beat the odds in so many ways, but I had only begun.

Graduation from high school was in the spring of 1985. A few months before graduation, my mother asked me if I had ever thought about getting a bigger bike. At that time, I was riding the 20-inch dirt bike that I did motocross races on. I told her, "Yes," but I could not handle the brakes on a road 10-speed bike yet. However, I had already been researching what kind of bicycles were available. I found out that they now had 'mountain bikes'; they were just coming out. I also found out that they had ten gears like road bikes, but the brakes were like those I had on my BMX.

The week before my birthday, a local Coast to Coast Hardware store had put out an advertising flyer, and it had a mountain bike in it for sale for $99. My parents and I went in and looked at it. It fitted me, so we bought it. Now my motocross days were over, but I still wanted to try bicycle racing. I set my sights on the Kelliher/Waskish Minnesota Wild Rice Festival ten-mile bike race. I wanted to start on a short race since it would be my first one.

The day of the race came, and three other local kids were registered. The race started, and two of the contenders who had road bikes took off. I was able to catch and pass the 3rd place rider. I knew that if I stayed in 3rd place that I would win three dollars. I figured that would be great for my first race.

About halfway through the race, I noticed that a car was following me. I thought that was strange. I did not know that it was the car that picked up the 4th place rider. He had gotten a flat tire. I told the driver after the race that I wish he would have told me that he was picking up the 4th place rider because I was worried that he was going to pass me up after I had passed him to get the 3rd position. I ended up getting 3rd place. I was happy. I finally found a sport that I was good at.

Shortly after that, my second ever road cycling race was held in my hometown of International Falls. It was a 24-mile race. I took 12th place out of 13 riders. I realized after that race that I needed a road bike. I knew I couldn't ask my mom and dad because they had just given me a huge graduation party at the end of May that year, and they had just given my grandparents a party that summer, so I knew I'd have to wait. Besides, college was next on my list of things to accomplish.

When the school year started in September of 1985, I walked into my first class at the Rainy River Community College. It was a little nerve-wracking because it was the start of my college education. Also, it was exciting because that day, I was offered my first real job.

I had wanted to get a real job when I was 16 in 1982, but instead of trying to find one, I just helped my dad mow the yard. We were going to take a trip to the state of Washington to see my dad's brothers and sisters, so my dad told me I could just help him that summer. I started looking for work the following summer of 1983, but I could not find anyone who would hire me. I had the same problem in 1984 and 1985. One of the main reasons was that I had physical disabilities. So, when I started classes at Rainy River, I was advised to sign up for work-study. I did, and that is how I got my first real job.

Brenda Crowe came to her husband, Scott Crowe's office where I was. She offered me the job of being a radio announcer. I thought that was quite crazy when she told me I was going to be a radio announcer. I looked at her and thought, "Mam, you must not hear too good." My speech is not good because I was born with a cleft palate, and all the surgery I had to repair it when I was two years old. But I thought, "If she is crazy enough to want me to try it, I might as well say yes."

I was looking forward to getting an actual paycheck. I was the Student Manager's Assistant in a way. They would put the new announcers with me first because I would not yell at them when they made a mistake. It was like having a second family there with us regular announcers. I worked there for the entire two years that I attended Rainy River.

College life at Rainy River agreed with me. The only hard part was the college counselor only got me 12 credits for my first semester. Because Rainy River Community College was just a two-year college, I had to overload my credits in those two years to graduate. I ended up getting 'burnt out.' I just barely made it.

Searching the sale ads that would come in the mail was a daily ritual. I was always hoping to find a good deal on a road bike. One night I saw an ad for a used ten-speed. I called the lady, and she said that she was asking ten dollars for it. I went to check it out the following day before my first class. It was just in okay shape, but for only ten dollars, I bought it.

When I got to the college, I was visiting with my friend, Steve Battalion, and he told me that he had a Schwinn Varsity bike that he would sell me for fifty dollars. Later that day, I went and checked that one out. I lifted it, and it felt heavy like my mountain bike. I knew Schwinn was a good brand, plus it was a 27-inch compared to the 26-inch Huffy I had at home. I ended up buying that bike also.

When I got home, I called my friend Brad and told him that I had bought two bikes, but I was unsure how to make them work for me. Brad came over and said that we would adjust the Huffy frame and use everything else off the Schwinn. That is what we did. There was still one huge problem. We weren't sure how we were going to make the hand brakes work. With my fingers fused together and them being shorter than normal, they do not bend. The regular road bike hand brakes would not work for me.

One day, a couple of months later, I was in my bedroom on my exercise bike and got an idea for the brakes. I quickly went and called Brad and told him of my idea. He told me that he thought he had even a better idea and would come right over. He said that since the brakes had dual levers on them, we could reverse them and flip them over, so the main lever faces me with the other on the inside facing down next to the drop. We just cut off the excess levers and put them back on. Now, all I had to do if I was going down a hill and I'm in the drops is take my thumb and push the lever down; otherwise, if I am on the hoods, I just must take my thumb and pull the lever back. I was pleased to now have brakes that would work. Now I could chase my racing dreams.

My Highschool Graduation Photo

Grampa Max Unger and Me 1987

1988 "Double" Deer Year

The 1989 Rifle Season in Minnesota

My bear hunt in 1991

4

Hunting and Racing

The 1985 Minnesota Firearm Deer Hunting season was approaching. My dad, mom, and I had gone and checked out our deer stands earlier that fall. For some reason, my mother was not going to hunt that year, so it was just Dad and me. Dad was going to use my mother's deer stand, which was the first stand on the trail. Mine was farther back into the woods. It was the first year I was using my grandpa's 30-06 rifle.

Opening morning, Dad and I headed to Kelliher, where our stands were. I dropped Dad off at my mother's stand and headed to mine. I climbed up into it and settled in for the hunt. Only a few hours had passed when I heard Dad shoot. At least I thought I heard him shoot, but it could have been some other hunter who was close by. It wasn't long, and I saw my dad walking down the trail to get me. He said he did shoot at a buck, but we needed to track it.

My dad is colorblind, so he needed me to spot the red blood trail. Dad cannot see the color red. It was challenging tracking because it had headed into a thick, tangled, bushy swamp. We finally found it and got it drug out. We went to the pickup for a break. Dad told me that he was going to make a drive towards me, so I headed back to my stand.

Dad went up the trail farther and headed into the woods to make a giant circle. Some time had passed, but then I noticed movement. It was a deer coming my way. I pulled up my scope and saw it was a buck with antlers. I pulled up my rifle on its front shoulder and pulled the trigger. The buck kicked into overdrive and headed towards the same low land that we just drug my dad's deer out of. I pulled up and fired again. Unlike the first shot, where I was calm, cool, and collected, I was excited now. Dad came back up the trail and asked me if I shot. I told him, "Yes." I told him that there was a blood trail, and we followed it. We soon found him. It was an eight-pointer. Then I got more excited because I finally shot my first buck, and it was a nice buck! My whole family was excited for me.

*

I was still working at KICC Radio at the Rainy River Community College in 1986 as a radio announcer. It was my first summer of training for bicycle races. The first Friday after the 4th of July, I headed to Waskish, MN, to spend the weekend with my grandma and grandpa. It was also the same weekend as the City of Kelliher and Waskish's Wild Rice Festival. One of the other reasons I was going there was to race in my fourth ever bicycle race. I knew I had a good chance of winning this time because it was only 10 miles long, and it was my second race for that year. I had taken third place the first time I did this race. I knew with a little bit of training that I could win. It was mainly just local people who signed up for the race, and they weren't serious cyclists.

My parents could not come because of other plans, so I asked my grandparents to drive my car to the finish for me. Grandma was glad to do it. I was feeling confident on the morning of the race, but as soon as I turned into the parking area, my heart sunk because I saw a car with four bikes strapped on top of it. I knew a cycling team had come to do the race and knew my competition just got tougher.

When I got out of my car, one of those riders came up to me. To my surprise, it was one of my old high school classmates, Dave Dahlen. He told me that the team had heard about the race and decided to join. They had a bigger race the next day. I told Dave that I had planned on winning that race that day, but now that they were there, I didn't think I stood a chance. I told them that about two miles from the finish line, a road went by a river that had fish in it. I suggested that they could stop and fish for a while to let me sneak by them and win.

Two other local riders showed up who I recognized from the year before. When it was time for the start of the race, one team member went straight from the gun. My friend Dave and another rider came up alongside me and started to help me 'ride the race.' In a few seconds, the other rider told Dave to get ahead of the local rider, then he told me to get behind that rider. That is the way we rode for about two miles. I was not appropriately dressed for this race. I had worn a sweatshirt and sweatpants, and I was hot. In the early stages of the race, Dave asked me how I was doing. I lied and told him that I was fine when my lungs were burning, and I felt like I was dying.

With about a mile or two left to go, Dave told me to go to the front. Then he got on my left side. The local rider was on my wheel. Dave's teammate was right behind him. I crossed the finish line first. I found out that Dave and his team did not officially enter the race and did the race just for something to do before their big race the next day.

My prize money was ten dollars. I took those ten dollars and bought myself a trophy, so I could have something to commemorate my first win in a sport that, despite my disabilities, I could do and excel at if I put my mind to it.

*

In the late summer or early fall of 1987, my dad and I headed out to our deer hunting area. We needed to find new spots to put our deer hunting stands. The first spot was just across a low area and on the edge of some cedar trees; this is where my stand would be. We went back farther and found another spot for my dad's stand. My mother didn't hunt again that year for some reason.

In the area where we built my dad's stand, uncle Curt and his brother, Jim, used to have stands, but they no longer hunted there.

A few weeks later, we headed to my grandpa and grandma's cabin in Waskish to get ready for the deer opener. My grandparents said they would sit in a gravel pit not far from the cabin on opening morning.

The next morning, we headed out to our stands. I was in my stand 30 minutes, if not a hair more before the sun came up. When the sun came up, it was quiet in the woods. I kept listening for sounds and looking for movement, but nothing yet. Then, suddenly, I heard my dad shoot. I figured he must have got his deer. But there was still nothing moving by me. A little while later, I heard my dad shoot again. I got frustrated because I was itching to shoot a deer. I hadn't been hunting that many years and I wanted to be as good as a hunter as my grandpa Max, my dad, and my uncle Curt. I decided that if anything came out, I would shoot. It wasn't long, and I saw my dad coming out of the woods. He had put two bucks on the ground. He said he saw a doe go by before the bucks so that he would put me on his stand.

Dad had a long walk out to the pickup because we couldn't park in the spot closer to our stands that year because the ditch had washed out. I got settled into my dad's stand, and Dad left. About 20 - 30 minutes went by, and Dad was just about to the pickup when I heard a deer coming through the brush. It was a buck. I pulled up my grandpa's 30-06, put the crosshairs on the front shoulder, and fired. The deer just ran off a short distance. A little bit later, I heard the brush crack behind me, and I looked to the right and saw another buck coming. Unfortunately, it either saw me or smelled me and ran off without me getting a shot off. That was the last deer I saw that day.

Dad came back from the pickup and asked if I shot. I told him, "Yes," and I got down from the stand, and we started tracking. We found it only a few yards away. We got the deer out of the woods and got it loaded. We went and found my grandparents and told them that dad got two and I got mine. We gave one of the bucks to them. When we got back to the cabin, Mom took a picture of my grandpa and me with one of the deer that dad had shot for my grandpa and a picture of the five-pointer I shot. That was the last year that my grandpa hunted. I have that picture framed, and it is on the entertainment center in my training room.

*

After community college, I transferred to Bemidji State University in the fall of 1987. There my advisor gave me two of the hardest classes there were. But I made it through with the help of extra credit. I got the chance to get even with one of the instructors of those tough classes. One of the male sororities had a dunk tank for a college spring event. Since one of the members was in my mass communication program, they convinced the instructor to sit in the tank. It took me two tries, but I finally hit the bull's eye, and he went in the water. I told him that was for the 'D' he gave me, and I dunked him again. I was content and happy.

In my first year at Bemidji State, I finished my Bachelor of Science degree in Radio/TV Production. It was either late April or early May when the 1987 Go Tour Bicycle Race was being held. There were two routes to pick from, 25 km (15 miles) or 70 km (42 miles). Since it was only my second year in racing bikes, I decided to do the 25 km.

I asked about the course layout and what roads were going to be used. I then started to add the course to my training rides. I found hills on it. I knew I could handle those because I am light and skinny.

Finally, the day of the race came. I told my parents, and they drove to Bemidji to watch me race. The weather was good that morning. I went and got checked in, then started my warm-ups. When the starter said "go," and we were off. I was feeling okay but nervous. This was only my second race that had a lot of riders in it.

I kept moving up the field and catching and passing riders, though I was never in the front group. I felt good, considering I was still new to the sport. I finally finished the race and found out that the awards ceremony would be at 1 pm in the commons area. I told my parents that they didn't have to go to the ceremony because I was sure I didn't win anything.

At the ceremony, I chose an empty table at which to sit. I wasn't planning on staying long, but an older male rider came and sat down by me. I decided to stay and give him support. He was an owner of a local business in Bemidji. I was glad I stayed because when they got to the age group of males 19 – 23 years, they announced that the third-place winner was me. I was shocked. I got up and received my third-place ribbon. Then I waited around for the 70 km results. That is when they called the guy's name who was sitting at my table. I congratulated him on his win as he did for me and my win. I took 3rd out of 7 total riders in my age bracket and 21st out of the 111 total riders in the 25 km race.

A few weeks before the July 4th celebration in 1987, I saw an ad for the Big Falls, MN Fourth of July Celebration list of activities. I saw that they were going to have a thirteen-mile bike race. I asked my parents if we could go so that I could race. I figured that I could probably do well with my capabilities, and I also knew that 13 miles is something that I could do. I had started doing 20–30-mile training rides at that time.

I'm not sure which road bike I had for the race. It was either the Huffy/Schwinn that my friend Brad and I built out of two bikes, or it was the Panasonic that my parents bought me for my birthday earlier that year.

It was the morning of the race; my parents and I loaded the bike into the car with my gear, and we headed to Big Falls. We got there early, and I got registered. The people at the registration told me that it is just an out and back course. It began in Big Falls and went to the river and back again. There were about ten riders who entered.

When the race began, I made it into the lead group with 3 or 4 others, and we took turns doing a place line. I was feeling good, for it was only my 3rd race ever on a road bike and only my 6th bike race ever. As we approached the turnaround point, I was in second place. The race volunteer made us stop so he could cross a line through our number to show that we made it to the turnaround. As soon as the first rider got his number marked, he took off. I couldn't go because they were in the process of marking mine. As soon as I could, I started chasing. The third-place guy caught up to me, and we agreed to work together to catch the guy out front. About halfway back, I pulled over so I could wave the next guy through. Nobody came by me, so I looked back and realized that I had dropped that rider. I could see the first-place rider but didn't have enough to catch him. I finished the race in second place, so I was happy.

One of the volunteers in the race knew my parents and told my parents that they were hoping that I would win. I did the best I could that day. Now things might have been different if they just would let us call out our numbers at the turnaround point, but it was the first race and the last race that they had.

*

I graduated from Bemidji State University in Bemidji in the spring of 1989, but I went back to BSU to do an internship at the public radio station (PBS) in the fall of 1989. Then it was official. I had my Bachelor of Science Degree in Mass Communications. I did some radio announcing on the college dorm radio station, but it wasn't as fun as working at the radio station at Rainy River. They had put me on the rock station at BSU, and I didn't know anything about that genre of music. Eventually, I started working at the college TV station; I also volunteered at the public TV radio station, running cameras. My family told me that they would watch the public TV station and feel proud when they would see the credits that said: "Cameraman – Shayne Stillar" at the end of a program.

After I finished college, I returned home. I had worked at the video arcade at the International Falls mall during my community college years and was able to get my old job back. Then later in the year 1990, I was able to get a job in the produce department for Super One Foods.

That fall, I had the chance to go deer hunting again. We lost our deer stands because the area we were in got logged off, but I had "freeways" of deer trails that went by my new stand.

We had snow on the ground that year, and we still had to go the long way around to reach our hunting area. Mom was hunting with us that year. Opening day was cold, but I was fine in my deer stand.

I didn't have an enclosed deer stand that year. I had just a platform with two railings and a seat.

I got there well before sunrise. As soon as it started getting daylight, I started checking and looking for movement. It wasn't long, maybe an hour or two, when I saw a deer coming up the trail from behind me on the left. This is not ideal for me because I am righthanded, but I have to shoot lefthanded because of my disabilities. The deer kept coming, not knowing I was there. It was only about 25 yards away and standing broadside. It made a good shot.

We had two doe tags that year, and I was sure I was about to fill one of them. I shot, and it wasn't long before Dad and Mom were there. We tracked it, and it didn't go far. We got it taken care of, and we walked back to the pickup to have a sandwich, and Dad and Mom had their coffee. I had hot chocolate. We then headed back to our stands. I made it to the trail and almost to my stand when I checked out the slashing, and there stood another big doe. It took a second or two to get my brain to focus. When it dawned on me that another deer was standing there, I pulled up my rifle and checked it out with my scope to see if it had antlers, but it was definitely a big doe.

I took the safety off and fired. It dropped right where it stood. I climbed up into my stand and sat on the floor, waiting those few minutes to make sure it was down. You don't want to walk upon a deer right away because it may run, or it could kick you. So, I waited and thought, "Great, now I have to go across the low swampy area again to get my dad and mom."

When I got out and started on the trail, my parents showed up and asked if I shot again. I said, "Yes, and I got a big doe." We got it dressed out and went and got our 3-wheeler and drug both deer out of the woods. I felt accomplished and happy because I had supplied my family with venison for the year, plus I was becoming a hunter like my dad, my grandpa Max, and my uncle Curt.

My first race in Big Falls, MN 1987

"In my senior year, one of my high school counselors tried
to discourage me from going to college.
He told me that I was not really "college material".
But just like the kids that bullied me when I was young.
I shrugged it off, and I just kept believing in myself."
~ Shayne

My parents, Jacque and Patrick Stillar and I at my
Graduation from Bemidji State University

BEMIDJI STATE UNIVERSITY
Commencement Ceremony
May 26, 1989

5

Broadsided But Not Beaten

Sometime in 1991, I received a call from WDIO television in Duluth, Minnesota. I went there for an interview and was offered a job as a production technician for the morning news.

I moved to Duluth, and shortly after starting my new job, I landed another job bagging at a grocery store in East Duluth.

*

In the summer of 1991, I decided that I wanted to try to shoot a bear. My grandma had shot many bears. The last one she got when she was 79 years old. My friend Steve Battalion hunted bear so did my great uncle Lyle Unger. I wanted to give it a try. Steve told me what I needed to do.

I sent a request to hunt into the lottery system. If I was picked, then I could hunt. My dad and I found a great spot to hunt on a corner of an old gravel pit just 12 miles from our house. Dad and

I built a stand and made a spot to put the bear bait. Steve told me to get a timer, so I would know when the bear was coming in. It wasn't long, and I could start baiting. I started getting a bear coming to check out my bait. The season opened on the first of September. I would go to the grocery store where I worked in the produce department. That is where I got most of my bait for the bear from the produce they were throwing away.

The first night I was out there, no bear came in, so I took more bait out to the stand the next morning. I found some evidence that the bear had been there, but it must have been after I left. I kept hunting every night and taking bait out in the morning. One day my mother cleaned out our freezer in the house. She gave me all the freezer burnt and bad stuff she wanted to throw away to use as bait. The next morning, I put out the first pail of this new kind of bait. I was excited because I figured that I would get bear in now.

That night I went out to our garage and got my hunting clothes out of the garbage bag that I had filled with cedar bows. I got into my car and headed to the stand. I was sitting in my stand when I heard a car or pickup driving up. A few minutes later, I heard a big bang. I figured it was someone who was out target shooting, but I didn't know in what direction. I got down out of my stand and walked out towards the vehicle. I found two men target shooting away from my direction but close to my car. They asked me where I came from. I told them, "My bear stand, across the road." They told me that they were about to leave, so I walked back to my bear stand. I spent the rest of the time in my stand in the dark.

The next morning when I went out with the last of the bait, I saw that the bear had come in again after I had left. I dumped the bait and went back home. That night I went out and got in my stand, hoping that this would be the night. I waited for about an hour when I saw something black coming towards me and the bait. It finally came into full view when it walked over a downed tree where I had a milk jug filled with grease drippings and suet tied to it.

The bear stood up on its hind legs, then got down, walked around the tree, and got back up on his hind legs again. That is when I decided to shoot because I did not know if something might scare it away. I aimed my rifle right at the spot my friend told me to shoot. I pulled the trigger, and the bear dropped down on all fours and went running straight away from me. I waited ten minutes and then got down and walked over to the fallen tree.

I went home and got my dad. We went back with his shotgun. We just walked about 20 yards, and there it laid. It must of went down even before I left the woods to get my dad. It wasn't a huge bear, but it was a nice one.

My parents had the hide made into a bear rug for me. I have that rug hanging on my wall in my training room. Dad took the meat to a processor and had sausage made. The sausage was excellent.

*

It was a few weeks before Christmas in 1991. I had worked the evening news running camera for the 10 o'clock edition. I only had about four hours of sleep that night, and I was on my way back to WDIO to do the morning news. I was scheduled to run the camera again.

I got up, got ready, and had breakfast. I was tight on time, but I knew I could still make it. I made it to the car in the apartment garage. I had two routes to take to get to work. One was to go up to 4th Street, but this particular morning I decided to go down the hill to 3rd Street because I knew the traffic lights would be blinking yellow, giving me the ability to slow down and proceed with caution instead of coming to a complete stop.

When I started to approach the first yellow light on 3rd Street, I slowed down and couldn't see anything coming. The next thing I knew, I woke up in St. Luke's Hospital's Emergency Room. I was lying in a bed with the curtain pulled shut around me. But there was an opening in the curtain, and I saw a cop who kept walking by and looking in at me. When he saw that I was awake, he came in and informed me that I was in a car accident. He said I was broadsided by another car.

A nurse came into the room and asked me if I needed to make some calls. I told her "Yes," and she got me a phone. I called the station first and talked with the morning news producer. She was great and told me not to worry. They had already received the news of my accident over the scanner and to just heal up and rest. She had a pleasant calming voice. I then called my parents and told them. They got ready and came to Duluth from International Falls.

The doctors ran tests on me and told me that I didn't have anything broken, though I did suffer a concussion. Then I remembered that I had unwrapped Christmas presents in my apartment for my parents. I called the station back after the hospital told me that I could leave. I asked if they could send the day person who ran errands for the station to come and get me. They did, and I had him take me to where my car was towed.

When I saw my driver's door smashed in a U shape, I wondered how I had survived and then end up without anything broken. I got what I needed out of my car and had the 'Day Errand Man' take me to my apartment. I then called my job at the grocery store on Woodland and told them that I was in an accident and would not be able to come to work that day. They told me that it was no problem, so I was off work from both jobs for a few days.

When I finally got back to work, I started having some back issues. Because of that, I stayed bagging groceries at the store for only a few months after the accident. My doctors advised me to quit bagging and carrying groceries because of my back pain.

I thought I better start looking for an attorney. My aunt and uncle told me about a friend of theirs in Hibbing that was the type of attorney that dealt with car accidents. I hired him to handle my case. First, he went after the other driver and won; then he went after my insurance because, according to Minnesota laws, he could. He won that case also. I was able to get enough settlement to get myself a new car, plus be able to put a little money away in savings. To this day, I still suffer from a bad back which is partly due to this accident.

I still do not know how the other driver got me out of the car. I had a Plymouth Horizon, and in it, I had my cross-country skis laying between the two front seats. My driver's door was not able to be opened.

During the big blizzard of Halloween 1991, I worked at the TV station all day. It was just me and one other production tech there to run the cameras when they had to do the weather updates and school closures. I was also working at the TV station when they had a big chemical spill in Superior, Wisconsin. I was there running the camera, floor directing, and running the teleprompter.

*

In 1993, I competed in my last Go Tour 25k Bicycle race in Bemidji. On May 1st, my parents and I headed to Bemidji so I could compete. I wanted to win the 25k before I competed in the longer race of 70k. My grandma Pearl Unger and a family friend, Donna Hodel, also came to watch me race.

I was racing for Loon State Cyclists at the time. I had tights and my team kit on. When we got to the Bemidji University, the weather had gotten colder, so I decided to put my good warm-up jacket over the top.

When it was time for the race, I got a position in the first row. When they said "Go,"- I made it into the lead pack. I felt good and did my turn at pulling up front. We just did short pulls. The pace was high. I was climbing well on the few hills that were on the course. It was not long, and we were back on the road that would take us to the finish. Unfortunately, on the very last downhill, my momentum carried me to the front of the race, which made the two riders who were with me speed up by me and up the hill to the finish line to take 1st and 2nd. I took 3rd. I don't remember how many riders there were in the race, but I think it was over 20. When we went to the reward ceremony, I found out that I took 1st place in the male ages 25 – 29. My mother got both the start and the finish of the race for me on video.

For Christmas of 1993, I bought my parents a gift which I bought with some special money. It started in May of 1993 when the Black Dog Road Cycling Time Trial Series began. I again started doing two separate classes. I did my division stock bike first class. Then after I finished, I quickly got back to the starting line, grabbed my second bike, and did my division in the aero class. It was basically a stock bike again.

The series started great for me in the stock bike class. I had started winning races for the nightly stock bike race. If I did not win first place, I was either second or third. I kept getting points.

At the last race of the series, I was the winner of the 1993 Stock Bike Division. I won $64 for my effort. I put it in an envelope and saved it until it was time to start Christmas shopping.

My parents had started going to Texas for the winters. They were going to be living in a motorhome, and they needed a VCR/DVD player. I went out and purchased them one for Christmas using the $64 that I had won. I then wrote a letter and taped it to the package. I wrote on the outside of the letter, "Read this first."

In the letter, I told my parents that this gift was bought with special money that I won for winning the Stock Bike Class. I told them that if it were not for them letting their 'special needs child' live a normal life and them encouraging me to chase my dreams, I never would have won that money winning the series.

At Christmas, at my Aunt Deb and Uncle Curt's house and my cousins, I had my mother open the letter and read it to herself. I didn't want her to read it out loud. Then my dad read it, then my aunt and uncle. My aunt Deb told me, "Wow, that letter was pretty special and great!" What I said in the letter was true. Because from day one, my parents treated their son, who had a rare syndrome, as normal as possible, especially when they let me race bicycle motocross. They knew that it was only a few years after I had my midface surgery and the doctors had told them that if I broke the plastic plate in my forehead, I would die. They never held me back and let me chase my dreams.

In January of 1994, I competed in the last mountain bike race my hometown of International Falls had. It was held on the frozen lake. It was a 10-mile course that Mike Budak, the race director, came up with. He used the ice roads that some car companies were using to test their new cars on. I was better prepared for this race than the other riders because I was doing a Duluth winter mountain bike race series. I had equipped my mountain bike with studded tires. I knew that my chances in the race were good.

I was racing for Loon State Cyclists. I told my coach that I was going to do this race in my hometown. He told me not to start out fast.

The Friday night before the race, my parent's made spaghetti for me to carb up for the race. The next morning, we loaded the bikes into the pickup and headed to where the race was held. I met up with Mike Budak, and he told me how the course was set up.

Dad and I drove the course so I could get the layout in my head. I also took my bike for a spin around the track. The track was about 2 miles long. When we got back from checking out the course, the other bikers started to show up. Not too many showed. It was one other father and son and one other single rider.

The sun was on our backs at the start. Since the track was short and the race was only three laps, I threw my coach's advice out the window. My plan was to go until I could not see any shadows of the two other riders I had seen as threats to my win. Once I was far enough ahead, I settled down into a brisk pace and one I could maintain easily. At the halfway point, I had a good lead. One other who I could see was there but in no danger of catching me yet.

I did the three laps and crossed the finish line in the first place. When I crossed the finish line, the other riders were nowhere in sight. The temperature that morning was well below zero, with a windchill of 20 below. I was in the pickup, warming up, when the other riders crossed the finish line. The other riders told their family members that they couldn't believe how fast I was. My mother told them that I had been competing in road cycling races in the summertime and trained the year 'round. I was glad that I could win the last winter mountain bike race that they held in my hometown.

While traveling to Virginia, MN, with my parents, I learned that they were having the Merit Days Cycling Time Trial Race in Virginia on that Saturday. I realized that I forgot my helmet, so I called Rich, a friend who worked at the Mountain Iron YMCA running the race and asked if I could borrow one from him. He told me not to worry, that he had one for me. I got to the Virginia/ Mt. Iron YMCA where the race was held, got my helmet, and registered for the race. I attended the pre-race meeting. When it was time to start the race, my friend Rich was the first rider out. I was a ways back in the field, but not far from first. There were between 15 – 20 riders.

When it was my turn, I started good and felt good. I quickly got into a rhythm. I began gaining on a rider in front of me. I was still gaining on him when I saw him turn. When I got to that intersection, I turned, too. There was no sign giving direction. They may have had a mark on the road, but my eyes and brain are slow to connect in a race. I had turned because I figured the rider, I was following knew the course better than I did. We came to another road, so I turned on it. Then my friend, Rich, who started before me, passed me. That is when I knew that I just goofed up – big time. I kept going as fast as I could. When I finally crossed the finish line, I went to the officials and told them that I goofed up and made a wrong turn. I told them I was following the rider ahead of me. I figured that I would be disqualified.

At the Awards Ceremony, Rich explained that two riders decided to do their own course, and the winner of the gold medal for my age group was me, Shayne Stillar. The other guy who I had followed got the silver medal. I was happy but still frustrated that I goofed up twice that day. However, it all worked out simply fine.

*

July 1994, right after my mother and her sisters threw a big wedding reception for my grandmother Pearl's second marriage. (She married Al Wooden. My grandfather Max died in 1991.) We took my cousins from Texas fishing on Red Lake. They caught a few fish. After the party, Dana and Chuck III flew back to their homes. I headed back to Duluth.

The next day I had a message on my answering machine when I got home from work. It was my cousin, Dana. He said that he wanted to take me on a fishing trip in the Gulf of Mexico. He said he'd get in contact with me later. When he called back, he asked me if I got the message. I told him that I did, but I could not go because my parents just put on the wedding reception for my grandmother, and we didn't have the funds to do that and that I couldn't afford to do that on my salary. Dana told me that I did not have to worry about paying for the trip. He said that he and his brothers and their father were going to pay for it. All I needed to do was to get time off from work. I told him that is something I could do. We made plans, and I looked forward to this adventure.

Dana sent me my airline tickets to Dallas and told me that he would pick me up there. We'd spend the night at his place then drive down to the Gulf the next day.

When I got to Dallas, Dana was there waiting. We headed to his parent's place in San Antonio. On the way, we stopped at the Texas Ranger's Law Enforcement Museum. That was interesting to see.

The day after we got to San Antonio, we headed down to Rockport, to my cousin Scott's place. That evening we went to a seafood restaurant. (That was back when I could eat most everything – before my hiatal hernia.) My uncle Chuck ordered raw oysters and asked if I wanted to try one. I said, "sure." Every Christmas, we would make oyster stew, so I kinda knew what to expect. It was good. My cousins were surprised that I ate it with no problem.

The next morning, we got up real early and headed to the Gulf. It was about five miles out to our first fishing spot. The boat was equipped with electric reels, so all I had to do was bait the three or more hooks and hit a button to lower the bait into the water. My cousins Scott and Dana told me how to bait and tell when I had a fish.

We were fishing for red snapper. It wasn't long before I brought up my first couple of red snappers. One of the deckhands came and got the fish for me, put our names on them, and placed them in a cooler on ice.

The boat would stay so long in one spot and move to another location in the Gulf. The boat held "The Biggest Fish" contest, so we all entered it. I went to reel in my fish at one of the stops, and it felt very heavy. When I got it to the surface, I found that my line was tangled up in several other lines. When the deckhand finally got all the lines untangled, they told Scott that someone on the other side of the boat just caught the biggest fish. Scott was frustrated because he said that due to the position of my rod, that fish was more than likely mine.

A short time later, Scott got seasick. They were all worried about me getting seasick. They hadn't prepared themselves and had forgotten that I was used to fishing large waves on Red Lake back home in Minnesota.

It was time to head to shore. When we got there, my uncle took my cousin Dana and my picture with our fish. I did okay, but it was not my kind of fishing with electric reels. Dana and I drove back to San Antonio while Chuck and Scott waited for the fish to be processed.

When we got back to my aunt and uncle's place, Aunt Maxine told us to go straight to the showers. When I stepped into the shower, the walls looked like they were spinning or moving, but I didn't get sick. That must have been the result of being on the boat for so long.

The following day, my aunt and uncle took Dana and me out for breakfast at a taco place near their home. My cousin Dana is over six feet tall and probably around 200 pounds. He told the waitress that he would have two eggs and potato tacos and two egg and sausage tacos. I told her that I'd have the same. Everyone was surprised that I ordered the same thing. I'm over 6' but only weighed around 145 pounds, but I was hungry. I was in full training for cycling then, and I could eat a lot.

6

Most Tenacious

I was reading an issue of one of my cycling magazines, sitting in my efficiency apartment in Duluth, when I saw a sidebar that stated that the United States Para-Cycling Coach was looking for riders. I thought, "Wow! Maybe I could qualify since I was born with Apert Syndrome and had severe physical disabilities." I wrote the coach a letter. A few weeks later, I got a phone call from the Para Olympic Cycling Coach. We talked for over an hour. At the end of the call, he told me that he thought I might be disabled enough to qualify for the team, but I would have to go through their doctor, who made the final decisions. I sent all my information on Apert Syndrome and pictures of myself to their doctor. He had also informed me that I would have to join USA Cycling. I did that the very next day.

For the next few months, I stayed in touch with their doctor and sent him information. During that time, I received my USA Cycling license and the race calendar for the 1995 racing season for Minnesota. I began to get mixed emotions because I saw that they planned to hold their Minnesota State Time Trial Championships while the Para Olympic Cycling Camp was held.

Being born in raised in International Falls, it was high school hockey that was the primary sport. I was always picked on, teased, and bullied when I was younger because I was considered frail and not an athletic person. This pushed me to achieve my dreams. Even though I wanted to compete at the Olympic level, I also wanted to do the State Time Trial Championship. I was doing well there, and I knew I had a shot at getting onto the podium. I had to fight through my insecurities and fear of starting something new.

While waiting on the decision from the Para Olympic doctor on my status, I decided to tell my friend, Mark Lennon, about maybe being able to do the next Para Olympics. Mark immediately said that I should quit doing the easy rides with the local riders and start riding twice a week with their cycling team. I said, "Okay," and the following week, I went to do my first ride with the team.

When I got there, another friend, Rod Raymond, was there and spoke for the team. He welcomed me there and told me that they knew why I was there. He also told me not to panic if I got dropped from the pack by them because they knew that it wouldn't be long, and I'd be able to keep up with them. Rod was right. I was dropped a lot during the first few weeks of riding, but my new friends never left me. One of them would always drop back to me and then help me catch up. If I couldn't catch up, he would not leave me until I knew how to get back to my apartment.

I was now able to enter more bicycle races. Before that, I was doing races on the Iron Range on weekends when they had one. I was doing well in the Northern Minnesota races. The first races I entered were sponsored by the Minnesota Cycling Federation and USA Cycling. They were run by one of the Twin Cities teams. These races were real eye-openers for me. They were tough, and I was just a category five or beginner's racer for USA Cycling.

I was still racing for Loon State Cyclists in 1995. I was training with the top riders in the Duluth area. I thought I was getting better, but I was struggling when it came to the bigger races.

One race I remember was either in the Twin Cities or western Wisconsin. I started out but eventually got dropped. What made me so frustrated was the president/coach of Loon State was standing near the start/finish line, so every lap I made, he saw me struggling. I felt terrible because I had been training hard, but it was not showing that I was.

I kept training and going down to the Twin Cities to compete whenever I could. Plus, I continued to take part in the races in Northern Minnesota as well.

One day I had the honor of being nominated for the Loon State Cyclist Most Tenacious Rider award. After seeing the other nominations, I figured I had no chance of receiving this. But just before Awards Night, after one of the races, the President/Coach of Loon State told me that I needed to come to the award ceremony. I asked my cousin, Stephanie Kemp, if I could stay that night of the awards with them, and she was happy to have me come. Stephanie asked me if I wanted her to go with me to the ceremony. I told her "No" because I was sure I wasn't going to win. So, I went by myself and sat with some of my teammates.

The awards were announced and handed out by the President. When it got to the Most Tenacious Rider award, they read all the nominees and announced my name as the winner. I was surprised. I walked up to accept that award with tears in my eyes. I was overjoyed because I knew that my teammates, along with the President/Coach, knew I had been training hard, and it hadn't gone unnoticed.

The Olympic doctor finally got back to me after several more phone calls. He broke the bad news to me. He told me that "Yes, I had severe disabilities, but in fact, I was too normal and in too good of shape to qualify for the Para Olympics." It was okay because now I could go to the Minnesota State Cycling Time Trial Championships. I was happy because it was the first big race of my career. I had the problem of getting to the race. The race was in St. Cloud, MN, 150 miles away from where I was in Duluth, working at WDIO TV as a production technician. Even though it was only a part-time job, it would be tough to get away.

My parents, who were usually supportive of me, started advising me not to go to the championship race. They were so far away, and not sure that I could complete this on my own. I was raised to respect my parent's opinions, but I knew, deep down, that I had a shot for at least the top 10, if not the top 5 if I was having a good day.

One night a week or two before the event, I called my first team, the Loon State Cyclist's president/coach, and told him that I was thinking about not going now. He told me that I should change my thinking because they would have a stock bike class for each category. A stock bike means a bike with no aero bars or disk wheels. The wheels must have 34 spokes. Right then, I knew that I would go. I knew now that my odds just got better.

It was a Saturday in early June, and I headed to St. Cloud for the Minnesota State Cycling Championships. I made it there okay, got registered, got my bike ready, and began to warm up. Soon it was time to get in line and wait for my start.

When I started, I had about a minute interval from the previous rider. I heard my count down, and I took off flying down the road. After I had gone a few miles, I noticed that my cycling computer said I was going 20 plus mph. I thought that maybe I was going too fast at the start and should ease up to make it through the 40 km course. I just kept going.

When I crossed the finish line, I looked down at my computer, and I saw that my time was just over 1 hour and 4 minutes. I felt okay about that and began my cool down. I caught up to my team president and another teammate. When I told them what my time was, they said, "Shayne, I think you placed." They told me that usually, the third-place position came in at 1 hour, 3 minutes something. I agreed that they were probably right, but I didn't let myself get too excited.

After the race, I had to drive back to Duluth because I had to work the 10 o'clock newscast that night. I went to check the posted results before I headed back. I looked at the USA Cycling category four stock class and saw that I didn't make 3rd place. I noticed that rider was 8 - 10 minutes behind me. Then I looked at the 2nd place winners and still couldn't find my name. The second-place winner was 6 minutes behind me. Then I went to see who took first place. Well, there was my name in the first-place position. I was ecstatic. A little while later, they gave me my gold medal. My three-hour drive back to Duluth and my evening shift at the TV station went great.

When I got home, I called my parents. Mom answered, and I told her to get dad on the phone. Right away, my dad assumed something bad had happened to me. I told them that they were parents of a State Champion now. Now the hockey moms and dads of International Falls had nothing over them anymore because now their son just won the 1995 Minnesota State Cycling Time Trials in the Category 4 Stock Bike Division. They were happy and proud.

Working for WDIO in Duluth as a cameraman

Filming Grandma's Marathon in Duluth, MN

International Falls Icebox Days 1995 for the Win

Presented with Most Tenacious Rider Award by Larry Martin in 1995

7

Old Goats

I was still working at the television station in Duluth. I started out working on the studio crew but was eventually moved to running morning audio. That was tough because the person who was training me would scream and yell at me if I made a mistake. I had trouble getting confidence in doing my job well. The pay was just over $4.25 an hour when I started. After four years at the station in 1995, I decided to go back to college.

There was a program at the Hibbing Community College. I was all signed up and had an apartment lined up, then found out that it was only a part-time course. I then found the water and wastewater operator program at St. Cloud Technical College. I talked with their recruiter and the Minnesota Department of Rehabilitation again and got help paying for my 2nd college experience. I turned in my two-week notice to WDIO TV sometime in the summer of 1995.

I started the twelve-month St. Cloud Technical College Water and Wastewater Operator School in July of 1995. The recruiter was not 100% truthful with me. He did not tell me about the mechanics and machinery repair that I would be required to do. However, both of my instructors were good to me. I also did my two internships that were required for the course. I had to get help with some of the more complicated math at the end of the course, but I made it through.

When I was a lot younger, I was mistaken for somebody else—the reason why is children and adults with Apert Syndrome look almost identical. But luckily, I knew about two of the young men that the person thought that I was. The first was when I was in Duluth working at WDIO TV. I was at a gas station when this guy asked me how I was doing. I said "fine," but then he told me that he remembered me from Duluth Denfeld school. That is when I knew he thought that I was the young man who was the first one in Minnesota to have the mid-face surgery done at the U of M Hospital. (I was the second person to have that done.) I explained that I was not who he thought I was, but I knew who he was talking about. He felt bad, and I told him that it was okay. I have had a few others that came up and asked me if I was someone they knew. I'd say to them, "No, but people with Apert Syndrome look very similar." They were understanding and told me they thought it was amazing.

There was one lady that was not so nice. I was going to St. Cloud Technical College and was at the St. Cloud Mall. I just walked into a store when a lady comes up to me, calling me another name. Since I had my back turned to her, I just ignored her at first. But then she got mad and tapped me on the shoulder and said, "I am talking to you!" I told her that my name was Shayne Stillar, and I am not who she thought I was. She did not believe me and kept accusing me of being the young man from St. Cloud who also had Apert.

I knew a guy in St. Cloud had Apert because his mother had contacted my mother one day. I was pretty sure this lady thought that I was him. I told her that I could prove my identity, took out my billfold and showed her my driver's license. She looked at it and said that it was fake and that I had it changed. I finally told her that I had to get going and that "I was who I was." That encounter ruined the rest of my day. I wished that I had been out in the mall corridor and not in a store when I had this encounter. Because I had a relative who lived in St. Cloud at the time, she worked just a few shops down from the store where this lady stopped me. If I was able to take her to her, this lady might have believed me.

Our family decided earlier that year that we would spend Christmas of 1995 in San Antonio, Texas, with my mom's sisters. That is where my mom's oldest sister, Maxine, and her husband, Chuck Davies, lived. They lived there ever since Uncle Chuck had retired from the US Airforce.

We were supposed to draw names for Christmas, but my cousin, Dana Davies, told everybody that he and his wife wanted my name for Christmas. I figured something was up. I had a feeling that my gift was not going to be store boughten or 'normal.' I knew my uncle Chuck had some hunting land which they called "The Ranch." I had already figured that my cousin Dana had something to do with hunting wrapped up in my gift.

My parents and I, along with my aunt Debbie and uncle Curt and their two girls, Steph, and Wendy, made it down to San Antonio, and when we got to Texas, no one said a word about the adventure I was about to embark on. I knew hunting was part of the trip because I was told to pack my hunting clothes and boots. I had figured it was going to be a wild pig hunting trip. When my cousin Dana picked me up, a couple of family members said, "Good luck hunting tomorrow!" Now I was positive that I was hunting, just not sure what I was hunting for.

When I got into the vehicle, Dana asked me if I wanted to know what kind of hunting trip, I was going on right then or tell me later. I said, "Now, would be good." He told me that he was taking me to a game farm in the morning to shoot an exotic goat. He wanted to know if I preferred to use my uncle's 30-06 or a 245 rifle. I told him that I shoot deer with a 30-06 and would use that one.

The next morning, we went to the game farm and met the guide. We got into the guide's pickup and started out looking for rams. It was not too long, and we spotted the herd. Unfortunately, I was not ready fast enough on the first sighting. I was not used to this type of hunting. Back in Minnesota, we sit in stands in the woods and wait for the deer to come by. Dana also told me on the ride out there that he wanted me to shoot the ram in the front shoulder and not shoot it on the run. He didn't want to chase mine as he did his a few years before that.

We caught up to the herd again, but again, I could not get ready fast enough to get a shot off. Dana told me that he wanted me to focus on the black ram at the end of the herd. We caught up to the herd again in an open area of the ranch. Dana then told me the black ram was at the back, so I pulled up; I put the scope on the front shoulder and pulled the trigger. They thought I missed because the ram was still standing, but the other goats had left. Dana told me to shoot again, but I was too nervous and was sure I missed it. Then the guide told me that I had hit the ram with my first shot. He said that I had made a 150-yard shot while the animal was on the run. Dana was proud of me. Oh, yes, I was thrilled also.

We got the ram ready for transport. Dana had a deer tag he wanted to fill, so we found a herd of deer. He told me to shoot, but I didn't have a good shot, so he shot and got the deer he wanted.

When we got back to the guide's house, we loaded the animals into my cousin's truck and went to the meat locker to get them processed. They had the black ram's head mounted for me. The goat I got was a Hawaiian Black Ram. It was close to being a new record. But that didn't faze me. What was important is that I got to go hunting with my cousin Dana.

Me and Cousin Dana Davies with the Hawaiian Black
Ram in Dec. 1995

International Falls Ice Box Days - January 1997

8

Getting to Know My Body Better

It was a few weeks before the 1996 Wild Rice Days Bike Race in Kelliher, MN. The race director had contacted me and told me that this might be the last bike race for this festival. My friend, Gerald Johnson, had also called me and told me that he would ride his tandem bike and asked me if I could be his co-pilot. Kelliher was like my second hometown because I had family there, and I told Gerald that I wanted to enter the race on my bike; he was okay with that.

My parents and I headed down to the Tamarack River cabin in Waskish the day before. On race day, I saw that my friend found someone to ride with him on the tandem. Only nine other riders showed up. At the pre-race meeting, the director announced that the tandem would not be eligible to win the race but could ride it if desired.

I felt good that day and when the race started. I took my pulls up in front of the pack, but I kept them short. My friend Gerald and his partner kept working on trying to get me. I was behind them. My dad had also entered the race, but he was off doing his own thing.

Just before the Waskish Post Office, I was on their wheel, and we all just kept doing a place in line. We led the pack, but around the 7–8-mile point, my friend attacked the tandem, and I quickly jumped on his wheel. Two other riders came with me. We kept going. As we approached the long gradual incline, I attacked and went as hard as I could. When we got to where the road flattened out, Gerald and his friend were alongside me, and I fell behind them. I figured that I would let them cross the finish line first since they didn't qualify for any awards.

Mom told me that they saw the tandem, then me, coming around the corner and got excited. I crossed the finish line in 2nd place (but it was actually first place). The race director told me that it was the last race for the Wild Rice Festival, and he felt it was fitting that it was the one that I had won.

*

While attending the college in St. Cloud, I saw an ad for Ginkgo Biloba, which is supposed to help with memory. I did not know then, but I know now that I made a bad mistake in going out and purchasing and taking that supplement. I took my first dose while I was attending classes and was still training for my bicycle racing. After a few hours after taking this supplement, I started falling asleep when I was away from class and in my apartment. I didn't get too worried yet, but it was getting frustrating because it affected my training.

My hometown bike race in International Falls was named "To Hill and Back." It was coming up in mid-August, and I wanted to do well because I had not won that race yet. I was still experiencing unscheduled naps during this time. I hadn't thought it severe enough yet to see a doctor. I did not know what was causing them. I headed home to do the race.

On the morning of the race, I arrived at registration and got my number. I then spotted one of my best friends, Jeremy Sartain. Jeremy told me that he would work for me that day because he wanted me to win this race. I told Jeremy that my training had been a little off, and I didn't feel great. I warmed up and got ready, and soon it was time for the race to start.

I made it into the lead pack and was moving roughly 20 mph. I was comfortable there and was just staying in the pack and out of the wind. We made it to Tilson Creek, where my parents were so that they could get a photo of me. I was still feeling okay, but that was to change in the next mile or two.

When we came to the first big hill in the course, we started to climb, and a rider attacked. Now I tried to go faster, but my legs suddenly went dead. I made it over the top of the hill, but the leaders in front of me were gone. I knew right then that my chances overall were also gone. I figured I could still place in my age bracket, so I kept going. As I got to the bottom of the hill and just before a sharp turn, I saw the leaders again.

Spotting my friend, Jeremy, and I hollered at him, "Jeremy, GO!". I went around the next corner and got ready for the next climb. I made it to the turnaround and shouted out my number to the race volunteers there. I then started up the next steep hill. I finished the last of the big Sha-Sha Hills and started back for the finish line. There were a few other riders still with me at this point. We went on the overpass over the railroad tracks. I knew the race would soon be done. When we cleared the last corner, I began my sprint. I did not win my sprint in my group, but I wasn't last either.

I found Jeremy after the race and asked him if he won. He said "yes" and asked me what happened to me. I told him that my legs blew on the first big hill. Though, I managed to get a medal in my age group.

When I got back to St. Cloud, I made an appointment to see a doctor. I explained to him how I felt tired all the time and told him I was taking Ginkgo Biloba. The doctor told me that I had chronic fatigue syndrome. I stopped taking that supplement. It took quite a few months, but I finally got my body back to feeling normal. I was so frustrated that I was so foolish in thinking something like that would help me, and instead, it made it so I had a rough race in my hometown.

I soon left St. Cloud and did a 3rd internship at a certified lab in Virginia, MN, after I graduated from St. Cloud Tech. The last instructor for the course knew that a lab job was a good option for me because I was good at doing the required tests. I took my Minnesota Class D Water Operator and Wastewater Operator test. I passed both on the first try. Now I had successfully graduated with my 2nd college degree.

Despite my achievements at college, living in a larger city, my heart desired to be home and in the woods. The outdoors is a part of who I am. I headed home for the 1996 bow hunting season for deer with a new career on the horizon. I had hunted a few times with my mother's old recurve bow, but with my stiff shoulders and crooked arms, I could not shoot far with it. I knew I needed to get myself a compound bow.

I talked to one of my classmates, he told me about a man he knew that sold bows in Aitkin. He told me that he might have just the right one for me. I called him and drove up from St. Cloud to his home. When I got there, we talked, and he showed me this left-handed bow. (I am righthanded, but I shoot lefthanded). We went out to where he had a target set up. At first, I thought that I made the trip for nothing because I was not strong enough to pull the string back. Then the guy told me to put the bottom limb of the bow against my leg and try to pull it back. I did, and I was able to do it. I let the arrow go, and it landed close to the bull's eye. I bought the bow and drove back to St. Cloud.

That fall, Dad and I went over to the other side of the land across the road from my parent's place in International Falls and put up by portable ladder stand. I went back home for archery deer hunting season. I went out the following morning to my stand and saw a deer right away, but it was out of range.

That night my mom had a nice dinner planned for us. She asked me what time I would be back to the house from hunting, and I told her about seven because that is when it got dark at that time of year. She said to me that we would eat at 8 o'clock. I went out late that afternoon to my stand and saw nothing. It was getting close to 7 pm with just enough light to shoot still, so I stayed a hair longer.

At 7:10 pm, I knew that I needed to start heading into the house. I climbed down and got on my 4-wheel ATV, and headed home. When I approached our property, I decided to turn and take the trail along our fence line. As soon as I did, I saw my dad coming down the trail. I stopped, and he said that there were deer at our apple tree. I grabbed my bow, and he grabbed my arrows. We quickly walked to the front of the house using the weeds, garage, and house to block our movement. We got to the front yard under my bedroom window. As I got ready, Dad peeked around the corner and said that there was a nice doe broadside under the apple tree. I stepped out and pulled my bow up and noticed that the distance was farther than I was used to shooting. I knew where to aim because I practiced shooting at that distance. I let the arrow fly, and I heard it hit and saw the deer take off. We went to the front door, and my mother came out. We told her that I hit the deer and we needed her to help us track it.

We found my arrow in the back garden. We walked down the trail tracking the deer. We didn't go far because there it laid. I had accomplished another goal in my life. I had taken my first deer with a bow and arrow.

Another hunting season, I don't remember what year, but it was the last weekend, and it had been a challenging hunt that year. Dad, Mom, and I hadn't shot a deer yet. My uncle Curt called a few days before that weekend. He told us that he was going to Kelliher to hunt last weekend and bring some friends with him. Dad and I decided to head to Waskish to our cabin and hunt the last weekend there. I drove up after work in Duluth. My uncle told us to meet him for breakfast before the hunt the next day.

Early morning, Dad and I went to our stands, and my dad got a deer that morning. I hadn't seen anything yet. We then met up with Uncle Curt and his friends. My uncle said he'd like to make a deer drive after breakfast. He was going to put me in his uncle's stand.

After breakfast, we headed out east of town to the meeting place. I got my rifle ready, and Uncle Curt took me with him. It wasn't long until we passed a stand. I started wondering where my uncle was taking me. We came to a clearing, or some call it a slashing. He told me to stand there and pointed out the direction from where the deer would come. He told me to shoot either doe or buck because he had doe tags to fill. He also told me to empty my gun, and then he headed off to his hunting spot.

A little time had passed, and here comes a doe doing "Mach 3". It was running away from me, but I took a shot and missed. A second later, a nice size doe came out and stopped about 30 yards from me. It stood broadside. I pulled up my gun and shot. The deer ran a short distance and stopped. I thought to myself, "How did I miss that one when it was so close?" So, I pulled up and shot again. It dropped. When I turned around, I saw another deer looking at me. I thought to myself, "Boy, you're not too smart to be standing there." I remembered what my uncle told me. I had one shot left in my clip, so I pulled up my gun and shot. The deer ran into the woods.

COURAGE IN THE FACE OF APERT | 75

A short time later, Uncle Curt and my dad walked up from where my uncle was sitting. They asked me if I shot. I told them, "Yes, there is one over there plus another one back in the woods." My dad told me that it made my uncle Curt smile. My uncle's brother took one of my deer, his friend took my dad's, and we took the one Uncle Curt's friend shot. I will never forget this hunt because I got to hunt with my dad and my uncle Curt Lundin.

*

In January of 1997, I decided to compete in my first cross-country ski race. The race was a part of the International Falls Ice Box Days celebration. My hometown is known as "The Icebox of the Nation." The morning temperature was 35 below zero Fahrenheit with a wind chill factor that made it feel even colder.

It was a 10km (or 6 miles) race and my first cross-country ski race ever. I had been competing in bicycle races for 12 years, so I asked myself, "what more of a challenge could this be?". My goal was to finish the race.

I bought myself some cheap goggles, and when I went to warm up for the race, my goggles began to fog up, so I elected not to use them. I had skied the first part and last part of the course earlier, so I knew it would be a risk for me doing the race without eye protection. I did not know what the middle part of the race held for me. I wanted to make sure that I could see any sharp turns at the bottom of any hills and couldn't risk being fogged up.

A gunshot signified the beginning of the race, and I started off feeling good. There were checkpoints along the course of the race, so I figured if a volunteer saw something wrong, they'd let me know. I made it past the last checkpoint, and nobody said a thing to me. I then got to a downhill in the course, and that is when my vision started to blur. I started seeing double. I fell going down that hill, but I got up and kept on going the best that I could. Before I got back onto the lake portion of the trail, I stopped to wipe my eyes.

When I started going again, that is when I saw the finish line. I had told my mother earlier to have my jacket ready for me when I crossed the finish. As I crossed the finish line, I saw my mother, and she told me to stand still because the local newspaper photographer wanted to take my picture. I had about two-inch-wide icicles hanging from my hat that were covering my ears. They went all the way down to my shoulders, and my eyes were iced over. It sure felt good to get my jacket on after all that.

I went into the resort lodge to get warmed and cleaned up, but it was difficult. My eyes were burning and were so painful because of them getting frozen over. But I was able to soothe them. Finally, I went out and found my parents. I told them that I had problems thawing out. They decided to bring me to the emergency room to get checked out. The doctor said that I had scratched the eye lens of my left eye. I was glad that it was just one eye. He told me that I would be fine, but to spend the rest of the day indoors.

When we got home, Tom Manka, the race director, called and said that I had won a medal. My dad went to their house and picked it up for me. I had won a silver medal in my age bracket. I was happy even though I was mad at myself for being crazy and doing the race without the proper eye protection.

*

In 1997, it was my last chance was to win my hometown bike race known as "To Hill and Back Bicycle Race" in International Falls. My training had gotten back on track. I had suffered the year before from chronic fatigue syndrome. I had been doing long training rides to get myself back into shape. I also rode the race's course several times a week.

I had been back home after getting my second college degree. I was also waiting to find a job in my new field. I felt good about my chances of winning the race, but I also knew there would be some tough competition.

The morning of the race came, and my parents and I drove to the starting area. The race time was earlier this year than in the past, which made the number of racers smaller because they had so far to travel. My friends Tony Carter from Grand Rapids and Greg Carlson from Hibbing were able to make it. I registered and got my number on, and then it was time to start the race.

It was a good start, and I made it into the lead pack. I was feeling good, and my friends, Tony, and Greg were with me. Plus, there was a rider from International Falls who was with us three. The four of us, plus a couple more riders, headed for the Sha Sha Hills. We made it to Tilson Creek, where my parents were waiting to cheer me on.

Shortly after, we hit the first incline of the hills. I made it up and over with the leaders, then soon after, we got to the bigger and steeper hills. It was just the four of us then. As I started down the last of the first set of hills and right before a sharp right-hand corner, I realized that my lineup for the corner was wrong, and I had to use my brakes a little. I lost Tony and Greg's wheels. I didn't panic because I knew I was a good time trialist. The other International Falls rider was still with me.

We worked together on the way back over the hills and back into town. I never caught up with Tony or Greg. We got to the final corner, and I'm not sure if it was the other Falls rider or me who went through the corner first. After we did, we started to sprint to the line. I'm not even sure which one of us crossed the finish first. It was close. The other Falls rider was built more for sprinting. I'm made more for climbing and time trials. My friend Greg Carlson took first place. I came in close behind and had a good race.

9

Bike Champion

This story starts in January of 2001 at the International Falls Ice Box Days Cross Country Ski Race. It would be the last cross-country ski race in my hometown. I had planned on just doing it for fun because I just had no-wax classic skis. When I was warming up for the race, a lady who was the news editor for the Falls Daily Journal newspaper approached me. She said, "Shayne, I know that I interviewed you last year, but can I interview you again?" I guess no one else wanted to talk. I told her, "Sure, no problem." I told her that it was a fun race, and I was using it for training for my summer bicycle races.

I had a good final ski race, and I had won a silver medal for my age bracket, so I was happy. After the race, I returned to Anoka, where I was living and working at the time. I kept training for the upcoming cycling season. My bicycle racing season started in April. In April, the road races began, and in May, the time trials began. My time trials were going well, and they were leading up to the Minnesota State Time Trial Championships, which I had my heart set on.

The morning of the State Time Trial Championships, I drove down to St. Peter. I arrived and got registered, then joined my friends and teammates. I started to do my warm-ups after I got my bike ready. The race started good, but after the turnaround, I started bucking a headwind. I was on my stock bike, my hand-built Creel, but it was just a regular road bike. I had no aero equipment. I fought hard and finished the 40 km course in a time of 1 hour and 9 minutes. Then, I did my cool down while I waited for the results to be posted. I found out that I had won my 3rd State Time Trial Championship for males ages 35 – 39.

The next time I went home to International Falls to see my parents, I had my dad take photos of me with my bike, team kit, and my gold medal around my neck. Then, when I returned to Anoka, I wrote a letter to the International Falls Daily Journal editor and included that picture with a bit of information about winning the State Time Trial Championships.

I did this as a bit of encouragement for myself since International Falls was known as a hockey town, and because I was picked on and teased so much when I was young, I wanted to show them that even though I couldn't play hockey - I made something of myself. I knew the odds of it getting printed were slim, but it made me feel good to send it.

About a week or two later, after work, I got a phone call from my mom. She told me they got a pleasant surprise after when they were reading the paper that day. She told me an article titled "Bike Champion" was above a photo of me with the information of my State Time Trial Championship gold medal. It made me happy because not only did it show that I was an elite cyclist and an athlete, maybe the ones who mistreated me when I was young saw it and then would know that their cruelty did not keep me down.

*

After I finished the water and wastewater operator training at St. Cloud, plus my 3rd and last internship at a certified lab in Virginia, I went back home to live and to start looking for work. I began to send out resumes whenever I got a lead on a job. I also went to the local job service and checked on their computers. One day at the job service, I saw an opening. So, I sent the company my resume. Within a week, I got two calls. One was from a town just south of Duluth that needed an operator. The other call came from a place in Anoka, MN. I set up both interviews the following week—one day at the one just south of Duluth, the other in Anoka on a different day.

On the first interview, I walked in and met with some of the town's officials. The interview went well until the water and wastewater supervisor walked in. He saw me sitting there and saw my physical disabilities. One of the other officials asked him if he had any questions for me. He said "No," and then they started talking about fishing and other stuff. That got me mad because I realized that I was just turned down for a job because of my disabilities. They finally told me that I could go and thanked me for coming.

I stayed at my cousin's house in the Twin Cities that night. The next day I went to Anoka and had my interview there. This interviewer was much better. The guy from the Anoka Plating Shop called me a few days later and offered me the job. I headed back down to the Cities and found an apartment. I worked that job for almost five years. When hard times hit the plant, they laid me off. It was five days short of my 5th Anniversary on the job.

It was back to looking for work again. I just started checking the job ads. I also went to the job service. I did get a few leads in my field, some of the others I was over-qualified for, but anything would pay the rent.

One day I was driving behind Walmart and saw a plating shop, so I stopped and went in to get an application. I took it home and filled it out and brought it back. Then, a few days later, I got a call from them. To find out it was the guy who was the head of the lab in the old plating shop I had worked at just a few months earlier.

At the interview, He told me that I had no experience in the position that he needed me for but was not worried about that. Instead, he said he wanted me to work there because he knew I was dependable and always on time, plus he like my work ethic. He also said that he had gotten other applications, but he wanted to hire me if I would accept his offer once he saw mine.

I did accept the job, but it started rough. I was not treating the hazardous waste like I did at the first plant, but I would be making the plating baths for the platers to plate their parts. Another reason why I said it started rough was that the young kid that was also in the lab making the baths asked me my shoe size. I told him nine and a half. He told me they didn't have any boots in my size. I did not think when he said that. I knew that the boots sometimes only came in whole sizes. I did get other safety equipment but no boots. So, I would be working with different acids and just wearing tennis shoes.

It was my first day on the job, and my nerves were tense. The first week went on. I had to go in early at the start of the second week. This young kid showed up late, so we lost about 20 minutes on getting this one plating line ready for the plater at 7 am. This one tank needed 6 gallons of sulfuric acid. I went and got one and a half gallons first and dumped it into the tank, but I needed another four and a half gallons. They had me using a 6-gallon pail with a screw-top lid. I assumed that it was safe. I put 4.5 gallons of sulfuric acid in it and went to the tank. When I came back to start on another tank, I noticed a trail of liquid that dripped out all along the walkway.

A few minutes later, I started feeling a slight tingling in my right foot, but I kept working. It kept getting worse. I went into the bathroom and took my shoe and sock off. There I found an area just under my right big toe that was all black. I washed it off and checked the first aid kit for burns.

At 7 am, my boss came in and showed him my foot and didn't do anything, so I kept working. I finally asked the young man if we were allowed breaks. He told me we were. So, I went and took five minutes and ate my lunch. Then at 9 am, he told me that I could go to Walmart to see what they had to put on burns. So, I rode my mountain bike to the Walmart just one block away. I was talking to the pharmacist, and then I showed her my foot. She told me that I needed to go to the emergency room NOW.

I rode my bike back to work and told my supervisor that I could either ride my bike to the emergency or they could take me. I guess I did have a severe burn. I got to the emergency room, and they made an appointment for me for the next day at Hennepin County Medical Center. As I was being discharged from the emergency, a nurse handed me a prescription. She told me that I could not drive for four hours after taking it. She explained that it was a strong pain medication. I then told her that I did not want it, and I ripped up the prescription. I told her that this pain was nothing compared to what I have endured in my life.

The next day, I saw the doctor, and the day after, they did a skin graph on my foot where the burn was. After I was released from the hospital, I stopped at the plant to get my first check on my way back to my apartment. The receptionist told me that I had to see the owner of the company.

When I walked in, he started chewing me out and told me that they would put me in another department until I was cleared to return to my original job. I told them that this accident was the company's fault because they should have gotten me boots right away, plus I was hurrying to cover for the young man who came in late. I also told them that I was raised to know that a person needed to try to meet a deadline the best as he could if there was one set. I also told them that the doctor told me I needed to take two weeks off. So, I would return to my original job when the doctor tells me I can.

I had started this job in the spring of 2003. I worked through the summer and into the fall.

Wild Rice Days 1997

10

As Long as I Can Fish

My parents told me that they had me fishing in a boat when I was only two weeks old. So, you could say that I was a born fisherman.

It took me until August 2003 to out-fish my mother, though. My mother held the record in our family of catching the biggest northern pike. My mom's parents owned a cabin on Upper Red Lake on the Tamarack River. The Tamarack River runs into Red Lake. So, my parents and I would drive from International Falls to their cabin the night before the fishing opener in May.

In May of 1987, my dad was up before me on opening morning. I got up at sunrise around 5 or 6 am. We fished for a while off the dock in my grandparent's yard. Then after breakfast, my dad, mom, and I headed down the river and out into the big lake. The trip downriver to the lake takes about 20 minutes.

We had just started fishing when my mother hooked a fish. It didn't take long for all of us to realize that it was a pretty big fish. I had guessed it was probably a northern pike. Thirty minutes later, my dad got the fish into the net and into the boat. My mother then announced that we were done fishing, and she wanted to head back to the cabin. I was not happy because I hadn't even been able to wet a line yet.

We headed back up the river to the cabin. When we got back, my dad weighed the fish, and it came to 16 lbs. We then heard that a tackle shop in Blackduck was holding a contest. Mom entered her fish in the contest and won first place. On that day, I vowed that someday I would catch a bigger fish than my mother's. My dad had my mom's fish mounted for her.

Now, I had caught many northern through the years, but I was waiting for that 'one day.' So, early in the summer of 2003, my mom, dad, and I went out fishing like usual. Mother said that she would drive the pontoon boat so my dad could also fish. Dad and I were fishing when I had a northern hit. I fought it and got it in the boat. It was a nice size, but still nothing close to the size of my mom's fish. I put my line back out and immediately got another good hit. That one was a twin to the one I just reeled in. That is when my mother said that if I ever got a fish bigger than hers, she would pay to have it mounted.

On August 30, 2003, my day came to fulfill my vow. I had to fight to get it. It almost wasn't my fish because my uncle Chuck Davies from San Antonio was in the boat right next to me.

It was very windy that day, and the water was choppy and rough. We didn't let that deter us. Chuck and I were fishing off the back seats without a bite for a long time when suddenly, my rod almost bent in half. I set the hook, and I knew I had a big one on the line. I told my uncle to take my rod because he was a trophy fisherman, but he refused. He said to me that this was 'my fish.' I fought and fought that fish. I wasn't worried because I was using my northern rod set up for the big ones. I just kept my line tight and the tip of my rod up. I finally got tired out, and my dad net the fish when it came to the surface and brought it into the boat.

When we got into the dock, we weighed the northern, and it was 19 lbs. I finally beat my mother's 16 pounder. Mom kept her word and paid to have it mounted for me. Now it hangs on the wall in the living room right next to her fish.

I eventually beat my record of 19 lbs. Several years after this fishing adventure, my aunt and uncle were back up visiting again. This time their granddaughter Taylor Davies was with them. This year, Upper Red Lake was closed to walleye fishing. My parents were gone somewhere, so I decided to take the little 14 ft. Lund out fishing for northern pike.

It wasn't too long, and I hooked a northern, about a four-pounder. I took it to my uncle Curt and Aunt Deb's cabin. Their cabin is on the lakeside and easier to get to from the open water. I put my fish on the stringer, went to visit with my aunt and uncle for a while. Then, I stayed for a time and headed back home.

Later that evening, I decided to head back out, and I asked my uncle Chuck if he wanted to go out with me. I let him use one of my poles. We headed down the river and out to the lake. I got hooked on a snag, so we lost some fishing time, and I told my uncle that it was getting late, and we should probably be heading back in. We decided to troll the mouth of the river and fish the river on the way back to the dock. When we got to the second marker in the river, and my pole bent in half. Again, I offered my rod to my uncle, and he refused again. The fight was on. This time the lake was a lot calmer, and the fish even jumped out of the water. After twenty minutes, I finally got it tired out, and my uncle got the net. I had to help my uncle with the net to haul this fish into the boat. We laid it in the bottom of the boat and headed to shore.

When my parents got home, they asked us how we did fishing. My uncle told them to look at the dock. Dad was surprised. He weighed the fish, and it weighed 25 pounds. When my dad asked me what I wanted to do with the fish, I told him, "Let's eat it!" So, we cleaned it and made a huge meal. It was great.

With living in Minnesota, I also had chances to go ice fishing. Uncle Curt called and asked if we could join them on an ice fishing trip to the Lake of the Woods in the Baudette area. Dad told him that it sounded like fun.

That Saturday, we got up early and headed for the Lake of the Woods. The Lake of the Woods is a vast lake that is on the border of Minnesota and Canada. It was still dark when my dad and I got out onto the ice. When we got to the spot where we figured it was close to where my uncle was, we got our fish house set up and four holes drilled.

The fish were on the slow side that day, but I stuck to it and continued to sit by my hole and jig my fishing pole. Suddenly, my rod bent in half. I knew I had hooked something big. I told my dad that it had a good fight to it. I saw the fish come up towards the hole, but my line was snagged around its fin so it wouldn't come up straight through the hole. I tried several times to ease the line to come off the fin, but it would not come. All this time, both Dad and I were watching this fish through the water. The closer it got to the hole, it kept getting bigger.

Dad went to the pickup and got the handle to the jack. It was shaped in a T. Dad reached down, and I let up the tension a bit, and between the two of us, we were able to get the head of the fish pointed up towards the hole so I could pull it through the ice. I reeled it in. It was a big one. When my uncle called us to see how we did that day, my dad told him that we got one big enough to mount. They were excited for me.

We didn't have a fish scale with, so we weren't sure what it weighed. We weighed it when we got home and found out that it was just a little over two pounds and wasn't a mounter. That was a let-down. But I told Dad we were looking at it for so long through the water that the water was magnifying the actual size.

The next day my uncle called, and Dad had to tell him that the fish wasn't as big as we thought it was. But, nevertheless, it was a fun day and a good trip.

*

In November of 2003, we went up to the cabin in Waskish, MN, for the opening of deer hunting season. It was just the start of Minnesota's Firearm Deer Hunting Season, and I got my deer.

Dad and I got two deer that season. I can't remember if I got both and filled my dad's tag or if he got one himself. I had taken a day off work to make the following weekend a long weekend. I had told my parents that I would come back home to Waskish to help him process the deer, at least get it skinned and quartered.

That Monday morning, I woke up around 5:30 am with a severe stomachache. I thought it might be one of my hunger attacks, so I got up and had a snack. But it did not help. I tried again, but I didn't get any relief. I began to get sick to my stomach. My parents were awake now, and I told my dad that there would be no venison for breakfast for me because I knew it would not stay down. I was dry heaving constantly by 10 am. I had my parents take me to the emergency room. It took the staff giving me four nausea shots and three pain shots to get my system to calm down. They kept me in the hospital overnight and did an ultrasound on my stomach in the morning. They thought it might be my gall bladder acting up. They couldn't find what was wrong, so they sent me to St. Mary's Hospital in Duluth for a week. They tested me and told me it wasn't my gall bladder, and they did not know what was wrong. They released me from the hospital without finding out from what the problem stemmed. I headed back to Anoka and went back to work. I needed to pay my bills.

I worked in pain and nausea for about two weeks. Finally, my parents came down, and we planned to take me to the Mayo Clinic. My friend, Dave Dahlen, who works at the Mayo Clinic in Rochester for their medical school, tried to get me into Mayo but was not having any luck. I asked my other friend, Jeremy Sartain, what hospital I should head to in the Twin Cities. He told me Regions Hospital in St. Paul was one of his choices. I was in too much pain to wait to get into Mayo, so we headed to Regions Emergency Room.

There they started running tests and thought I had malrotation of the intestines. They kept me in the hospital for a week. It was there that they discovered that I was born without a gall bladder. Luckily for me, the chief surgeon assigned to my case never felt confident in the test results to the problem. So, he never opened me up.

While at Regions, my mother called my supervisor at work and kept him updated on my condition. He told my mother that he had people at the plant telling him to send me home because they could see that I was in some significant discomfort, but he also knew that I needed to work. He had just left the decision up to me when I could not go on anymore. So, regions released me, and I went back to work.

After the first of January of 2004, my parents came down to Anoka; we headed to the Mayo Clinic. They ran daily tests on me for a month but never figured out what the problem was. So, in February of 2004, I headed back to work.

I got a pleasant surprise when I arrived. The safety person told me that I was being moved to waste treatment. I was happy because I still had to work with acid in my new position, but now it was just a few acids I had to work with, so that was good. I found out a day or two later the reason why I was moved to waste treatment. It was that I was doing some of the jobs that the platers were supposed to be doing. I did not know that at the time I was doing them.

Some of the platers had worked at the first plating shop that I was at, so they knew that I had a good work ethic and was new to making the baths.

I started getting trained in on their waste treatment operation. I also received a better respirator to wear when I had to empty the sludge from the sludge dryer. In the first plant, I just had a paper mask to wear. Here, I received a respirator with canisters. I even wore it if I had to move a shipment of chemicals from the loading dock to the storage if people were smoking in the loading dock area.

This position lasted only until June 29th of 2004 because that was the week I broke my hip in a weeknight criterium race at the Dakota Technical College in Rosemount, MN . (I'll tell you about this in the next chapter.) After I healed from that, I returned to my new waste treatment job in October of 2004. It was then that I started to have pain in my right shoulder.

Shortly after I returned to work, I got chewed out again by the plant owner. The state had come in and fined them, and waste treatment got cited. The whole plant had many violations. My supervisor told me that he did not tell the owner that I was on medical leave because he figured I might have a problem with that.

I started seeing the shoulder doctor. I pushed to have the surgery for shoulder replacement because my insurance deductible had been reached for that year, so I knew that the insurance would cover nearly 100% of the surgery; plus, I could not bear the pain anymore.

*"My parents
told me that they had
me out fishing in
a boat when
I was only two weeks old.*

*You could say that
I was a born fisherman."*
~ Shayne

11

An Elite Cyclist

In late 2003 or early 2004, at one of the Black Dog Road Races in Burnsville, MN is when I had two teammates from an opposing team try to scare me with "crash talk." I was sandwiched between them, waiting to start the seven-mile time trial course. I was doing the stock bike class, which meant I had at least 34 spokes in my wheels, plus no bars on my handlebars. These two other riders from the other team were trying to scare me by saying that I had no chance against them. They were on stock bikes also. I looked at the rider in front of me; I thought, "I don't need to worry about him." Then I looked at the guy right behind me; he did concern me a little. The rider in front of me finally started, then 30 seconds later, I started.

It was not long until I had my 'prey' in sight when I took off, and I passed him within the first mile or two. I think I caught and passed a few other riders, too, and no other riders passed me. The rider who I was concerned about was the rider behind me. He was the one who was trying to scare me before the race began. However, he never did catch up and pass me.

I know what these two riders were thinking, that since they could see that I had deformities, I couldn't be a strong rider. I saw these same two riders two weeks later at the next Black Dog Road Time Trials, and this time I got right behind them at the registration. As soon as they saw me there, they said they did not want me behind them. So being a sport, I got out of line and went back three riders behind them. Hopefully, these two riders learned that you couldn't judge a book by its cover.

While I was still living in Anoka and working as an environmental technician in 2004, I managed to do a few time trials. My parents came down from International Falls and headed to St. Peter for the Minnesota State Time Trials Championships held there.

I got registered for the Male Master 35- 39 Division but would be riding a stock bike. I got word that multiple Olympic and World Champion Jeannie Longo of France was there. She had been in the Twin Cities to do a pro bike race. I was busy getting my bike ready and getting my pre-race warm-up in. I was feeling good about my chances. It was time to get in line and wait for my turn to start. In time trials, riders are released thirty seconds to a minute between each other.

Making it to the turnaround was easy. The way back was a bit harder because I was battling a headwind. Stock bikes have more wind resistance than aero bikes. But I made it to the finish. I got cleaned up and was waiting for the times to be posted. I wasn't feeling too good about the race. Then I saw Jeannie Longo standing not too far away from me. I went over to talk to her. She asked me how I did in my race, and I told her that I didn't think my time was too good. But she said to me that she thought that I had done rather well by my unofficial time according to my computer. She admitted that the conditions were tough that day for everyone. That made me feel better. I had my dad take a picture of us together because it's not every day you get to meet an Olympic and World Champion. She treated me with respect and as an elite cyclist despite my disabilities.

They finally posted the results. My time was 1 hour and 3 minutes for the 40 km. I placed 6th out of 10 in my age bracket. Even though I was the only stock bike in this class, I didn't receive a medal because the Cycling Federation decided to take away the stock bike class. Jeannie Longo's time was 56.06 minutes, so I did not do too bad because she just beat me by just under seven minutes.

*

June 29th, 2004, I was heading to the Dakota Technical College in Rosemount, MN. I was going to race in the last of the criterium series for this location. The weather was great that night. I entered the race for the USA Cycling Cat. 4 riders. I do not remember if I entered other races that night because sometimes, I did two races in the evening. They were only short 10 – 15 lap races.

Considering that I had just gotten off from work, I made it to the race site in decent time. I signed in and went to get my bike ready. I had plenty of time to get in some warm-up laps before the race. I found out that they reversed the course that night to change things up slightly since it was the last race; this made the S turn section come up quicker on the track layout.

When it was time for the race to begin, I lined up and got into the pack of riders for the 12-lap race. In-circuit races or criterium races, I try to play it safe. That is due to my bone structure which is not normal.

Apert Syndrome greatly affected my bone growth, and I knew my limitations. When the S turn section would come up, I usually stayed to the back of the pack to give me an extra margin of safety. This night's race was going well for me because I stayed with the group for the whole race with one lap to go. I played it extra safe in the S turns.

When I came out of the S turn, I was all alone, no other riders around me. So, I had a quick thought, "Tonight, I'm having a good race."

I began to contemplate the next daytime trials and knew that I was leading the stock bike series for that race. I figured that if I caught up to the group, I would end this race on a high note. So, I popped it into high gear and took my bike up to 30 mph. I was beginning to gain on the group. Finally, I caught up to them on the last big wide sweeping right-hand turn. I had too much momentum, so I had to take the inside lane where there was more room. Everyone was going wide on that turn.

That's when it happened. A rider right in front of me got cut off and had to hit the gravel, and he went down. I had nowhere to go, so I went down too, right over the top of the first rider, then the rider behind me went over me. I hit hard and was in extreme pain on my right side. For me, the pain was manageable, but I knew something was not right.

My best friend Jeremy and a member of our team got to my side. Jeremy asked me if I could walk, and I told him that I didn't know yet. With the feeling I had, I kinda doubted that I could. He had three other riders get me up slowly onto my feet. Jeremy told me to try and put pressure on my right leg. I did for a second and realized that wasn't going to work. So, they laid me back down. One of the riders asked Jeremy if they should call an ambulance. Jeremy told them "No" because he knew ambulance services are not always covered by insurance, plus he knew I already had an ambulance bill I was still paying on from my car crash a few years earlier.

They loaded me into the back of one of the race official's cars and got me off the course. Then they transferred me into Tom's (a teammate's) car. My other teammates grabbed my things from the race area and then drove me to the nearest hospital. Jeremy drove my car to his parent's house after the race.

When we got to the hospital, Tom went into the hospital to get help. The nurse came out to get me with a wheelchair, but she went back in and got a gurney when she saw how bad I was.

They admitted me, and Jeremy and his dad got there after dropping off my car. They got me to x-ray and found out that I had a broken hip. Jeremy called my parents back in International Falls and told them about what happened. They drove all night to get to the Twin Cities. Jeremy and his dad went home because we were told that surgery wasn't going to happen until later the next day. My parents got there about 6 am the following day. I told them about my crash and that I needed to have surgery for them to fix my broken hip.

My mother was holding a piece of paper in which she had 5 of my bikes listed "for sale." I corrected her and told her that I had six bikes, and none were for sale. She had assumed I was going to be done riding bikes. I did say to my parents that I wouldn't do mass start races anymore. I would just do time trials. I also told them that I was going to start running. I decided to do 5 km runs or shorter. I also told them that I was going to start swimming so I could do triathlons. I'm not sure what my parents thought about that.

Soon the orthopedic surgeon walked in and introduced himself. He told me that they would try to do my hip at 3:30 that afternoon. But because of a full schedule and a meeting he had to attend, it might be later.

My cousin Wendy came to see me, and she told my parents to go to her townhouse to get some rest, and she would stay with me until surgery. They began to prepare me for surgery at about 3 pm, but they had to take me back to my room after a while because the one in surgery ahead of me was taking longer than expected. Finally, about 5 pm, they came and got me to continue to prep me for surgery. The surgeon came to see me and apologized for everything taking so long.

The surgery went well, and after it was done, the surgeon told my parents that he had never seen so much muscle in a person's leg as he saw in their son's leg. But unfortunately, I had lost a lot of blood during surgery because of my syndrome, so I had to have a transfusion that night.

The following day, the surgeon came to see how I was doing. He apologized to me again for cutting so much of my muscle. I told him not to worry and that he just answered a huge question I had been wondering about - I had always wondered if I had made it to the "elite" cyclist level. What the surgeon told me confirmed to me that I had, so no apology was necessary.

He told me no riding for 12 weeks. When I saw him three weeks later, I asked him if I could use my bike on the trainer. He asked me if I could fall off it, and I told him, "No." I told him it was locked in and rock solid. He agreed it would be great therapy for me but to not over-push myself. I assured him that I wouldn't. Later that day, when I got back to my apartment, I got on the trainer and did 1 mile in 15 minutes, and I was just barely pedaling. I was happy because now I could have something to do again that I enjoyed very much.

12

Duathlon? Why Not!

Early October of 2004, I was about to see the orthopedic doctor who had put a plate and three screws into my right hip earlier that year. A week before my appointment, my right shoulder started giving me problems. I started having severe pain, and it was making my job as an environmental technician extremely difficult. My work was treating the hazardous waste for the plating plant in Fridley.

I called my hip doctor and told the staff that I wanted x-rays taken of my right shoulder. They took x-rays of both of my shoulders but said to me that he didn't work on shoulders, but he had an associate who did. I made an appointment with him. He tried giving me a shot (which I didn't take), and then he ordered physical therapy.

That didn't seem to help, so my parents and I decided to get the surgeon to replace my right shoulder. With me spending all of January of that year at the Mayo Clinic in Rochester and then my broken hip in June, plus my chiropractic treatments, my insurance deductible had been reached. So, for it to be covered, I needed to get the shoulder replacement surgery before the first of the following year.

I got the surgeon to agree that a shoulder replacement would be best. It would be my 30th plus surgery of my life. I was to find out that it would be a difficult one – pain-wise. Even though my pain tolerance is a least 4 points higher than average, I was getting older.

The surgery went well, but the surgeon wasn't prepared for what he found when he got into my shoulder. He discovered that my shoulder was not 'round,' he found out that it was square, but my socket was round. So, I had been experiencing 'bone on bone' pain for quite some time. After surgery, the surgeon told my parents that he did not know how I lasted this long with enduring the pain.

I did have some minor complications recovering in the few days after surgery, but nothing I hadn't gone through before. The doctor came into my room and gave me the bad news that now I couldn't return to work. The information didn't bother me too much. I was not real happy working there anyway, and the owner in the past mistreated me. The problem was nothing that I did, but what they did, and I didn't feel good about it.

After Christmas of 2004, I headed down to South Texas to recover in good warm weather with my parents to their retirement park.

*

When we got back to Minnesota from Weslaco, TX, I tried pulling back my compound bow. I couldn't, so now I knew that I better get myself a crossbow. I sent in to get my permit that I needed to get a crossbow. I began looking for a crossbow to purchase. I found one within my budget in an old sporting goods store in Bemidji. My parents and I went to look at it. The owner of the store was great and let me try it out. I purchased it and right away began practicing.

That fall of 2005, I went out and sat on the field, but after a morning hunt, I found a note on my car from the property owner. The message stated that he had a better place for me to hunt. So, I stopped by his house on the way home, and he took me to one of his other fields where his sister saw many deer the night before. I walked around it and found a spot to sit that evening.

When I went to that spot later that day, I saw deer on the other side of the field, but they were way too far away for my crossbow. When it was getting close to sundown, I started stiffening up, so I put my crossbow down and stretched a little. That's when I heard the brush crack, and suddenly, a doe stepped out onto the field, then another, and they were in range. By the time I picked up the crossbow, they had moved out of range again. I didn't get anything that night.

The following day, my dad and I went back to that field and found another spot, close to where I was the night before, to build a stand. We made one of our simple stands there, just a floor, a railing, and a seat. That night I went to that stand just before the sun went down. I said a little prayer to my grandpa up in heaven to give me a little help. It was not long after, and I heard the brush crack, and a little later, a deer stepped out and stopped right on my 20-yard mark. I carefully took the safety off and pulled up, aimed at the front shoulder. I pulled the trigger and heard the arrow hit. I called my parents, and they drove in to help me track it. It got too late, so we decided to continue the tracking in the morning.

The next morning, we got back on the trail of the deer. It was leaving little sign for us to follow, but my mother was a good tracker, and after several hours, my mother found it. It was a nice eight-point buck. My dad found a trail and started to go back to get the pickup and 4-wheeler. Luckily, my uncle, Curt was up and was just coming into town, so he gave my dad a ride to our pick-up.

We drug the deer out. I was excited that, even though I may not have made the right shot that I needed to put the deer down right away, I was able to get my first deer with a crossbow. I was thankful for my mother that she found the deer. I have the antlers up on my bedroom wall yet today.

My biggest buck was a nine-pointer. I'm not sure of the exact date, though I remember that my mother did not hunt with us that year, though she did come to the cabin with us.

My dad and I got up early on opening day and started off to our stands in the dark. We settled in, and the sun started to rise. It was quiet, and nothing seemed to be moving. I kept alert and kept moving my head to make sure I covered all directions. About an hour or so after sun-up, I looked across the slashing, and I saw movement. I pulled up my rifle and saw that it was a deer, and it had antlers, though I couldn't count how many he had, which didn't matter because I hunt for the meat, not the trophy. I waited until I could get a clear shot. I aimed and pulled the trigger. The deer hit warp speed and ran roughly 100 yards away from me. I called my dad and told him that I shot at a deer but was unsure if I had hit it, though I felt that I did.

About 15 minutes later, my dad was at my stand. He told me to stay there but to motion with my hand to show him the direction the deer ran. I wondered why he wanted me to stay in the stand, especially since I could see the blood trail and he couldn't because he is color blind. But I did as he said. Dad worked one trail and then another one. When he got back to my stand, he told me that he found it and that I had shot a nice buck. We then went together to get it ready for dragging. The area we needed to drag it through to get it out was wet, and it was too early to run a four-wheeler. We left it at my stand while I went back up into the stand and continued hunting.

The deer was a nice 9-pointer. It could have been considered a 10-pointer, but one prong was too short to be called a 'point' legally. We processed the deer when we got home, and my parents had the head mounted. It is still in my bedroom, and it was the last buck I shot with a rifle.

*

Since I promised my parents in July of 2004, after my hip surgery, that I wouldn't compete in any more mass start bicycle races, I decided that I would just do cycling time trials. But I wanted to add to my routine, so I started running, along with swimming. I wanted to be able to compete in triathlons.

I had started doing short runs in 2005 at my parent's place in their retirement park in Weslaco, Texas. I also kept doing my daily rides on either my road or mountain bike. When I started running, I just started out doing short distances because I was unsure how my body would react to running.

When I got back home to Minnesota at the end of April, Jeremy Sartain advised me to come down to the twin cities. He told me that I needed to go to the running store that he uses to get a good pair of running shoes. They would make sure that I got the right pair for my feet. My feet are not normal. My five toes are fused and webbed together. On the bottom of each foot, I have a huge bone sticking out. He knew how vital the correct shoes were for me. I went to the Twin Cities and got the right shoes. They immediately increased my run mileage.

My first and only duathlon was in July of 2005. A duathlon is only a run, then a bike ride, and then finishing with another run. I had started searching for duathlon and triathlons to take part in when I got back from Texas with my parents at the end of April. I saw they were going to have a duathlon in Bemidji in July.

I knew that it was going to be an experience since it was my first multi-sport event. It included a two-mile run, in the beginning, then a 10- 12-mile bike ride, and then another two or three-mile run to the finish. I had no expectations because I had just started running when I was down in Texas that winter.

I arrived at the Bemidji High School, where the event was held. One of the organizers showed me the mount and dismount line and where I could rack my bike. When I started my run, I eased myself into it since it was my first run. It went okay, but when I came to my first transition from running to biking, my bike was the only one left on the rack. I got my shoes on and got my bike past the mount line and took off. It was not long when I started catching up to and passing riders. I eventually caught and passed one of the other males in my age division.

The bike leg went well, as I knew it would, but the transition from biking back to running was slow. My legs started cramping up on me, so I had to walk a little. I finished and was happy with what I could do and got my first one under my belt. Then the male rider who I passed earlier came up to me and told me that he thought he was doing good but changed his mind when I caught up to him and passed him like he was standing still. I apologized and told him that I had been bike racing since 1985 and won a few time trials. He told me he thought I was awesome. That made me smile. My total time was 1 hour and 6.20 minutes. I placed third in the male 35 – 39 age division.

After my right shoulder replacement in 2004 and having my surgeon telling me that I couldn't work anymore, I went down to Weslaco, Texas, with my parents to recover. Those four months from January to the end of April were tough. I had my mountain bike, but I had no idea where to ride. So, before I headed back to Texas with them in October of 2005, I researched the internet, trying to find a fitness center. I found one and called. They told me they had winter Texan rates.

When I got down there, I called them again and found out that they offered spinning classes. I made an appointment with a personal trainer who worked there. I went in to meet Jacob Adams. In conversation, I told Jacob that I was a competitive cyclist. He told me he knew a few riders who had started a riding group in Weslaco. He told me that they rode Saturday and Sunday mornings. He invited me to join them that Saturday. He also said to me that his girlfriend was the spinning class instructor. So, I started the spinning classes with the girlfriend twice weekly.

That first Saturday, I went to their meeting place, and that is where I met Mr. Mike Givilancz, Mr. Alberto Garza, Mr. Jamie Rodriquez, Mr. Steve Kelly, and Mr. Charlie Wood. They gave me a friendly welcome, and we had a great ride. Our first ride together was to Blue Town. I had ridden around 50 miles by the time I got back to my parent's park.

I rode with these guys for several years after that, but then Jamie moved to LaFerria, and Charlie moved to Harlinson. But Albert kept riding with me after the group broke up. Mike also rode a few times over the years. Mike's sister, Tricia Givilancz, started to ride with Albert, and his future wife, Olga Garza-Guadiana, started doing new routes to either Mercedes, LaFeria, and Harlinson, Texas.

I continued running, cycling, and swimming when I could. The next running race would not be until 2006. I did the Big Bog 5km run in Kelliher, MN. I finished the 5km in 23.01 minutes. I won in my age division. I also took 5th out of 32 runners/walkers who entered. I realized that I needed to get more miles on my legs.

*

During 2006, I was able to take in a new experience. I got to see an oyster bed. My parents and I traveled to Rock Point, Texas, where my cousins Scott and Laura Davies have a home. Scott and his son took Dad and me out fishing in the Madre for red drum and speckled trout. But the fish weren't biting that day. It was my first time casting and trying to "pop" the line as I reeled it in. One of the spots we were fishing was right next to an oyster bed. It was like a little island made entirely out of oyster shells.

We saw something lying on the oyster bed; it was a huge alligator. We were in casting distance of the gator, so my cousin cast a line with just a bobber on it, over the top of the gator's tail. Well, we woke him up, and he quickly got into the water, and we quickly put the boat in gear and got out of there.

We didn't catch any fish that day though I had fun. I hope that my cousins will come to Waskish, and I can take them out on Red Lake to fish for walleye and northern pike.

Me and some of my friends in Texas - Albert, Chris, Olga, Erick and Tricia

13

Running the Race

Foster parents Clara and Pete Reiners raised Dad along with their eight children in Mizpah, MN, but he was able to connect and maintain a relationship with his natural family who lived in Spokane, Washington. We traveled to Spokane when I was young and visited them, and they came to Minnesota on occasion to visit us.

My cousin on my dad's side, Tom Sipp, and his wife moved to the Dallas/Fort Worth area. It had been 33 years since we have seen each other, so I decided it was time that I flew to Dallas to visit them. We made the arrangements, and in early 2006 I boarded a plane. Tom picked me up at the airport, and we spent the evening visiting and catching up with the news of our families.

Tom was a marathon runner, and since I couldn't get on a bike for my daily spins, I asked him if I could run with him the next day. I told him I probably could only go three miles since I hadn't pushed myself beyond that distance. He decided we'd run some trails he usually took for his morning runs.

The following day, we got up early. It was cool for a Texas morning. When we got to the trails, I let Tom lead because he knew the way, but I stayed right on his heels. About the halfway point, I got tired of following, so I sped up and passed him, but we remained close together. Tom told me he was surprised at what a good runner I was.

After our run, we met up with his son Kevin and wife in Fort Worth and went to a place to eat known for their great fajitas. We all ordered the combination platter. I was hungry. Not only did I eat every bit of mine, but I also finished off everyone else's food as well. When I got done, my cousin Tom said, "Shayne, I had no idea what to expect from you since I have not seen you since you were seven years old. But this morning, you ran my legs off, then passed me like I was standing still, and now you out ate all of us. You don't look like you could eat that much."

The next morning, they took me to church with them, which was great. The church had electric guitars, drums, and a keyboard to back up the songs. We enjoyed the rest of the day by relaxing and visiting. I have only seen my cousin Tom and his wife one time after that, but we stay in contact by phone and email.

Today, my dad is the sole survivor of all his siblings, natural siblings, and foster siblings. I wish their children would come to Waskish so I could take them fishing on Red Lake.

*

One winter, while my dad and I were ice fishing on Red Lake, we met an orthopedic doctor. We saw this airplane flying low as he went over us. Pretty soon, it landed, and the pilot got out. He started talking to my dad. When my dad asked him what he did for a living, he told him he was an orthopedic surgeon. My dad told him that I needed my left shoulder replaced and that it was a unique case because I had Apert Syndrome. This doctor told my dad that he had experience with Apert, so we decided to see him for the surgery.

The plans for my surgery were put on hold when my mother was diagnosed with stage four esophageal cancer about the same time. I knew my dad couldn't handle the stress of both of us needing medical care. For the next few months, we dedicated our time to my mother.

*

I rode my mountain bike over to my aunt and uncle's house on a summer day in 2006 when a pickup backed out of a driveway. I must have been in his blind spot. I hit the side of the pickup. I didn't think I was hurt but later realized that I was injured worse than I first thought. I ended up with a broken rib.

My local doctor ordered several tests, and one was an upper GI endoscopy. The doctor who performed it was the same doctor who found my mother's cancer. He told me that there was an area that made him concerned. I had intestinal health issues and suffered from indigestion and pain. He sent me to a Natural Pathologist who helped me find some relief for my problems. But it wasn't until 2016 when they finally figured out what I was dealing with.

In August of 2006, I did my second running race. In the neighboring town of Northome, they held the Scenic Sinkhole Scramble. It was a 2-mile run/walk or a 5km run/walk. I decided to do the 2-miler. I took 7th out of 100 participants and took 1st in my age bracket. My time was 15.25 minutes.

Training always was an everyday necessity. My next running race was the following year at the next Scenic Sinkhole Scramble in August of 2007. I placed in the top three for my age bracket. I think it was first place again. I placed 8th out of 129 runners.

In July of 2008, I did the Big Bog 5km race again in Kelliher. My time was 24.44 minutes, and I took 3rd in my age bracket. Then I did the Scenic Sinkhole Scramble again that same year. My time for the 2-miler was 15.23, and I took first again in my age bracket.

Then it was back to the Big Bog race in Kelliher and my time for the 5km was 25 minutes, first in my age bracket and 7th out of 20 runners. I did have to walk a bit in this one. Then back to the Scenic Sinkhole Scramble in 2010. A runner in my age group gave me a hard time at the start of that year. When he saw me next to him, he said, "Oh great, you showed up. I wanted to win in our age division this year." I told him that I had broken a rib a month before, so I might not be too good today. I told him to "just do your best." My time for that 2-miler was 15.31 minutes. I placed 7th out of 77 runners. I didn't do too bad considering that I got boxed in for a few yards, but I tried to be patient and get myself out into an open area. I was able to set my own pace. I took 2nd that year. I saw the runner in my age bracket just ahead of me the last half mile, but I couldn't close in on him. I missed first by 16 seconds.

I entered the Scenic Sinkhole Scramble two more years, in 2011 and the other in 2012. I came in either first or second, both years. I did some running training in 2013. But just before the 2013 Scenic Sinkhole Scramble, I had my first vertigo spell. My doctor told me no traveling on the weekend of the race. Then my physical therapist advised me to stop running and swimming altogether because it was hard on my back. It was discouraging, but later I was able to achieve a dream I had since 1984. Now I had something new to work towards.

*

I continued with the Cycling Time Trials during the time I was running. In June of 2007, it was time for the Minnesota State Cycling Time Trial Championships in St. Peter, MN. Since my mother was diagnosed with esophageal cancer and was battling that, it was hard for me to leave her and go to the time trials, but I felt I needed to. I needed to deal with what was happening in my own way. I needed to be with my friends and teammates.

I drove down the Friday before and checked into a hotel. Then I rode to the race area and pre-rode part of the course. I had an excellent warm-up ride. Afterward, I went and had dinner and a good night's sleep.

In the morning, I ran into some Bianchi/Grand Performance teammates by the hotel's front desk. I was able to talk to the Bianchi Rep, Brent Cohrs. Brent didn't know that I'd be racing yet, and he was genuinely friendly and respectful.

When I got to the race area, I got ready and started my warm-up. I realized then that I had a huge problem. My right hip was so sore and stiff that I could hardly walk. My warm-ups were challenging, but I did the best I could. When it was time to start, Jeremy Sartain, one of our elite team members, was volunteering as a holder. He asked me how I was feeling. I told him that my right hip was off the charts for pain. When it was my time to start, I went as best as I could with the hip. After a few miles into the race, the pain in my hip went away. I was so glad.

I made it to the turn-around for the 40 km and started back. It was going well until roughly the 16-mile mark; that is when my left shoulder started to ache extremely bad. I knew that shoulder needed replacing, but I knew that it had to wait. I did the best I could for the last 8 miles. When I finally saw the finish line and crossed it, I was in tears. I quickly wiped my tears away so nobody would know how much pain I was in.

A few seconds after crossing the finish line, I saw my friend, Bonny Donzella, she asked me how the race went, and I told her, "Ok." She could tell something was wrong and asked what was wrong. I told her "Nothing." She told me that I didn't seem like myself, and she knew something was up. I finally admitted to her about how tough a ride I had and then crossed the finish line in tears due to my left shoulder. She understood.

I went to cool down, then headed back to the car. I went to a church that was letting us use their facilities to get cleaned up. While I was in the men's bathroom, the Bianchi Rep, Brent Cohrs, came in. He saw me in my team kit of the St. Paul Bicycle Racing Club/Bianchi Grand Performance Team that he sponsors. He asked me how it went. I told him that the start was rough due to my right hip being in pain, making it hard for me to walk, let alone ride a bike. But I told him that it went away after 3 or 4 miles, then the last 8 miles, my left shoulder hurt so bad that I crossed the finish line in tears. I also told him that despite everything, I thought everything went ok. He was supportive and told me to come out and stop by his table when I got done.

When I stopped by his table, he handed me a Bianchi T-shirt and thanked me for riding Bianchi. I told him, "No, thank YOU for sponsoring our team, especially our elite teams." I left his table feeling awesome. I hadn't met Brent until that morning, and now he gave me support after the race, plus giving me respect and treating me as an elite rider just like the rest of my teammates. My disabilities didn't seem to be that big of an issue at that moment.

My time for the 40 km race time trial was 1 hour and 2 sec. I placed 7th out of the 11 riders in the male 40 – 44 age bracket, and I did it on a stock bike. I didn't get any medals for that time trial, but I did ok for what I was dealing with. Knowing my mother was not well and battling cancer at home made this time bittersweet for me. It was my best time for the Minnesota State Time Trial Championships.

14

Tough Changes

I'm not sure what year it was that I got my first real computer, but I decided to search the internet and look up Apert Syndrome one day. I wanted to try and find other people with this syndrome and maybe somehow reach out to them. I felt that I had a lot of experience with Apert and thought perhaps I could help someone else deal with it.

There was a posting from a family in the eastern part of the United States. They had a daughter with Apert and had made a website for her. I sent them an email, and the father wrote back. He asked me to send pictures and a paragraph or two about myself. He wanted to make a web page for me. He told me about a support group page for families who had Apert in their family.

I immediately sent them pictures and my information and joined the support group. It was not long after joining the group when I found a family that didn't live far from me who was part of the group. They invited me to a picnic that they would go to with other families who had kids with Apert or a similar syndrome.

Attending that picnic was tough on me. Being with these kids brought back memories of what it was like when I was their age, but it was good that I went. The parents were able to ask me questions about what it was like living with this syndrome. The following year, one of the mothers had the gathering at their home, and I went. After the party was over, I was able to have a long conversation with the mother who hosted the event. She thanked me for taking the time to talk to her privately. I was glad that I could give her some hope for her son.

When I first joined the Apert Syndrome support group, I had a family from British Columbia contact me. They told me that I was the reason why they let their 8-year-old daughter, who had Apert, compete in a kid's triathlon. I know that ever since I first joined that group, I have had the opportunity to help others going through what I went through.

Once I had a father from the Philippines tell me that I give him hope for his child. He said he goes through pain when other people make rude comments or pick on his son. He has been able to share my story with others to help them understand.

I have had families from all around the world tell me that my story has inspired them and give them hope. I have heard from families from Australia, New Zealand, Russia, Egypt, Canada, plus many states in the United States. These families inspire me, too. They give me the reason to go on and chase my dreams and to continue to inspire those who need an encouraging word.

I have realized that children and adults with Apert Syndrome are not the only people my story has inspired. My national cycling teammates and World Champions have told me that I am an inspiration to them. They have even said that I am 'incredible' because they are healthy and able-bodied and find what I do difficult. Being called 'incredible' is not something I thought I would ever hear. They don't know how I manage to train with artificial shoulders or when my piriformis causes me so much pain. They are also amazed that I can continue if my back is out of line or if I have dry heaves in the morning, that I can force myself to get on the bike or the trainer and get a ride in that day.

I have had a few friends and former classmates tell me that I have been an inspiration to them because I keep moving forward even though I may be having a bad day.

My daily training is necessary for me. I have my dreams to reach and goals to achieve. To me, my current and past teammates and my cycling friends are my inspiration. I have professional cyclists from national and from other countries that I follow. Those I know personally are my real heroes because they do not see me as a person with disabilities but as a normal person and an equal.

*

In the early morning of September 25, 2007, I woke up at 4:40 am. My alarm didn't wake me; I just woke up. Then my dad came rushing into my room, and he was crying. He asked me to go with him because he told me that he thought my mother had passed away. I went out to the living room with him and went to my mother. I checked for a pulse and couldn't find one. She felt cold, and I knew right then that I had lost my mother. I was deeply saddened, but I also knew that she was not in pain anymore. Her suffering was over.

I lost a strong ally that day. She had fought for me when I was young and in school. She made sure my teachers did not give me any special treatment that would tag me as disabled or incapable. She and Dad treated me as a normal son, and she wanted my teachers to do the same. My third-grade teacher, Mrs. Kjellgren, told me how my mother helped her teach kids with special needs.

My mother was a great mother. She was also a great nurse when she needed to be. I remember once when I was into bicycle motocross, and I took a nasty spill in our driveway. I went into the house and locked myself in the bathroom. My mother was canning vegetables from her garden, but she knew something was wrong. She kept insisting that I let her in so she could see what needed to be done, so I finally let her in. She looked at my injuries and told me that I needed to go to the doctor, but I had to wait until she finished the batch of canning she had on the stove.

She was supportive of me during my life. I think that I had only been in bicycle racing a few years when the new clipless pedals came out. She told me that she thought I should get them so it would make it easier for me. So, I ordered them, and she was right.

My mother worked most of her life. She took a few years off and didn't work when I was young but returned to working full-time when I got older.

She was diagnosed with esophagus cancer a little before the year 2006. When my dad and mother came home and gave me the news, it hit me hard. I knew that sometime during that year, I would be losing my mother forever. We were very close, and I knew it would be a hard thing to go through.

That year was extra difficult because of the pain in my left shoulder, which started to worsen. The pain level was above my threshold. I knew I needed to have my shoulder replaced, but I couldn't have it done when my mother was sick. I would have to wait and put her needs first. I wouldn't leave my dad to have two patients to care for, so I just continued to do my training and learn to manage the pain the best I could, with just over-the-counter pain meds.

I hated seeing my mother suffer, especially when we got down to Texas. I don't believe the doctors down there did all they could have to help my mother. We had our last family Christmas with my mother's youngest sister and her family before leaving for Texas that year.

It was tough in Texas. I feel the Texas doctors took a different approach than the ones in Minnesota. Her doctors in Minnesota were doing well. I knew my mother's cancer was terminal, but Texas's care did nothing to help my mother. When we returned to Minnesota in the spring of 2007, they were able to get back to her doctors in Bemidji and back on the plan that was working for her to help relieve her pain. She did well during the summer of 2007, but I knew she was getting worse.

In September of 2007, her cancer really got bad. They had to put her on hospice. They brought a hospital bed to our home and set it up in the living room. She wasn't in hospice long until she passed away.

I tried being strong for my dad, so I didn't let myself grieve too long. I dove into cycling to keep myself going.

On the day of my mother's funeral, my dad told me to have my friends, Brad and Jeremy, sit at the head table with me so I would have both family and friend support. Brad is like a brother to me, and Jeremy was a good friend. On the day of my mother's funeral, we found out that Jeremy and I were also cousins.

It has been thirteen years since my mother passed away. I miss her daily, but I know that she is with me in spirit even if she is gone. Since then, I have had some big wins in the cycling time trials and finished two triathlons in her memory.

Everything I did after my mother died was a bit different. After my mother was gone, I still went hunting, though now without my expert tracker. I had not seen any deer for a few years following my mother's passing, but I finally got lucky one year.

This particular year, my dad and I made a secret trail to my stand so I could use the trail for the morning hunt. I had decided to do a morning hunt that year, but the wind was not really in my favor. I made it to my stand before sun-up. I climbed into my stand and settled in. A few hours passed when I heard the brush crunch, then it crunched again, and I could tell it was coming my way from straight behind me. That meant that whatever it was, it was coming downwind from me.

I slowly turned my head around, and I saw two deer. I froze and just kept my eyes on them. The one knew that something wasn't right but wasn't enough to make her run. The bigger deer kept moving towards me and was 20 yards in front of my stand. I took the safety off my crossbow, took aim, and pulled the trigger. The deer ran off. I called my dad and told him what I shot. I got down out of my stand and found my arrow. I could tell that I did hit it. My dad showed up, and we found the deer. It was a spike buck. I was happy that I finally got a deer again.

A few days later, I was doing an evening hunt. It was about 6 p.m. I said, "Ok, Mom, I know you're in heaven with your mom and dad, but if you could please push a deer out to me tonight so I can get a deer for dad, and we can finish the deer season. I want to get back to training on my bike. Oh, Mom, you have twenty minutes to do this because I would like at least thirty minutes of daylight left in case I needed to track it." I kept my eyes open and searched the area. All-of-a-sudden, as I turned my head around, I spotted a deer. I froze still again. The deer moved slowly towards me and stopped about 20 yards away. I pulled up the crossbow, took the safety off, aimed, and fired. I called my dad, and he came, but before he got there, I got down out of the stand and tracked it myself. It had not gone far. It was a doe. It was probably the sister or girlfriend of the buck I shot two days before. It was my first double deer season with my crossbow with my mom's help.

*

One week after her death, she somehow let me know it was time to get my left shoulder replaced. I was awakened at 2:30 in the morning one night in extreme shoulder pain and missing my mother terribly. I knew it was time.

That day my dad and I went to Bemidji to try and find that doctor we had met on Red Lake ice fishing. We found a doctor with that name, but it wasn't the same man. It was a different man with the same name. When I went in to see my nurse practitioner, she told me that she knew who I was talking about and knew him. Her staff made me an appointment with him, and luckily, they had an opening the following week.

The doctor's office was in Bagley, so that is where we went. After I saw him, he told me that he had an opening for surgery the next week, and they set up a pre-op physical, so they got me an appointment in the Blackduck Clinic for the next day.

A week later, I checked into the hospital in Fosston and went into surgery to have my left shoulder replaced. It all was happening so fast.

My left shoulder was in worse condition than my right shoulder was. I think that is because I had crashed my bike in 2004 and I think I broke my collar bone. I didn't tell anyone about it at that time. I never went to the doctor. I just put up with the pain because I didn't want to miss any work.

The surgery went well, and the doctor didn't have any problems, but the recovery was tough at first. I would ask the nurses for pain meds, but when they would come into the room, they wouldn't believe I was in pain because I wasn't showing any emotions or signs of distress. I was so used to living with extreme pain that I guess I didn't respond as other people did. This went on for a couple of days. Finally, a nurse noticed that I was experiencing pain by looking me in the eye. She talked to the other nurses to see what options were to help relieve the pain. I tried to come up with a plan on my end too. The nurses finally started working with me. We were able to get the pain under control. I finally was able to start eating and was able to get discharged.

I was not off my bike for too long afterward. It was only a few weeks later, and I could get on my trainer. My shoulder healed up well, but to this day, I still have bad days where my left shoulder is off the pain charts.

In 2008 I started having issues with my stomach. I went and saw a gastric doctor in Weslaco, Texas, and found out that I had a hiatal hernia. Because of that, I had to stop eating some of my favorite foods. A few of the items that I had to cut out of my diet were fried fish, deep-fried shrimp, tomato-based sauces, and garlic. There are many other things I had to cut out of my diet, but these were the first things. Up to this point, there was nothing that I couldn't eat. I've never been a fan of vegetables. I only eat peas, corn, carrots, green beans, and squash. For fruit, I only eat bananas, green grapes, and pineapple. But I could eat and do eat almost everything else, even the food from the "doggy bags" that my parents would bring home for me after they were out for an evening.

I can still put away the food when I want; I just have to be pickier about what I eat. People are amazed that I am 6 feet tall and skinny. I try to consume 3,500 calories a day, but it is usually more, especially on training days. I burn between 500 to 1500 calories when I train.

When I left home for good in 1991, my parents were happy because their food bill was cut in half. My mother always had to cook enough for six people when I was home. I've learned to cook for three because that is how much I eat when I'm training.

Getting my hiatal hernia fixed is an option for me, but my grandpa Max had a hiatal hernia that he went to the doctor to have resolved, and he still had problems. So, if I watch what I eat, I do fine. I've had enough surgeries; if I don't have to have one, I choose not to.

15

Why Not Triathlons?

After I recovered from my bike crash and broken hip in 2004, I started training to do triathlons, just like I told my parents. That meant that I had to start running and swimming. The swimming leg was the first leg in a triathlon, and I knew it would be my most challenging. The only swim stroke I can do because of my bone structure is the breaststroke. My artificial shoulders do not work well with the crawl or freestyle stroke.

I started to run and swim when I could. Late in the 2000s, when I was down at my dad's Texas winter residence, I had heard about the Wet n' Wild Sprint Triathlon. It was a 300 m swim, a 13-mile bike race, and a 3-mile run. On March 20, 2010, I did my first Sprint Triathlon in Corpus Christi, Texas.

On the first leg, the 300 m swim, I did not do as well as I had hoped. It is different to swim in a 25 or 50-meter pool than in my dad's retirement community pool, which is not designed for swimming laps. My swim time was 11 minutes and 44 seconds. My transition from the swim to the bike was also problematic. I had to go about 50 yards in my bare webbed feet. But once I got on the bike,

I got into my rhythm and started passing other athletes. My time for the bike was 37.57 minutes, which was the third-fastest out of 9 male athletes in the male 40 – 44 age division.

The bike to running went a hair better. My body tired in the run, so I had to run, then walk, and then run until I finished the 3 miles. My time was 33.08 minutes. (11.02 pace per mile) and my total time was 1 hour and 28.07 minutes. I placed 64th overall and 6th out of 9 in my age division.

I missed the 2011 race due to either injury or weather, but I returned in 2012. That year went better. After my first triathlon, I knew how I had to train to get ready for it.

On March 18, 2012, I returned to Corpus Christi for my second Wet n' Wild Triathlon. This time I came better prepared for it. I had been swimming more, and I also brought along sandal crocs so I would have something to put on my feet to get to the bike race after the swim. I even brought a 5-gallon pail so I could sit on it while putting on my cycling shoes.

Before the race started, as we were waiting for our swim starts, I started chatting with two other men in my division. When it was time to start, I wished them luck. My swim went better this time, and my time for the 300 meters was 10.47 minutes. The exit from the pool was more manageable because this time, there was a ladder for us to use. My crocs helped, and I made the transition to bike much more effortless. The pail to sit on helped some also. The bike storage place was small, so space was limited. The bike leg went well, and my time for the 13 miles was 38.03 minutes. The transition from bike to running went better also.

My 3-mile run went quite a bit better this time. I ran the whole distance without any walking. But as I was about to enter the finishing chute, a young woman volunteer stopped me and told me that I had to keep going. I told her that I didn't and that I had already done the 3-mile run and it was time for me to cross the finish line. She finally let me enter so I could finish. I was frustrated. I knew that she saw my physical disabilities and didn't think there was any way I could have already done my 3 miles. I also knew that there was no way she could have known that I was already an elite athlete, and I knew what I was doing.

I got nice compliments from the two men I was talking with before the race. When I was getting changed into my street clothes, I heard two voices talking to each other and coming my way. I heard one ask the other, "Did you see that guy go by on the bike? He went by me like I was standing still." The other guy said, "Yes, me too!" Then they saw me and said, "Shayne, we thought that we were having a good bike leg, but when you went by us, you made us look like we were standing still." I said thanks and even apologized for passing them. But then I told them that I was a cyclist and a time trial specialist, so the bike leg was my strongest event. They thought that was awesome. It made me feel good. I finished with a time of 1 hour and 23.37 minutes. I don't know what my run time was because there was a malfunction with my chip. This triathlon was my last.

After returning home to Minnesota, it was June; I loaded up my bike and made my way down to St. Peter for the Minnesota State Cycling Time Trial Championships. I would be racing the stock bike class again. I'm not sure if my dad was with me or not that year. Sometimes he came with me, and other years I made the trip solo.

Upon arrival, I made my way to the church parking lot to register. Our team was putting on the race, so I was able to visit with some of my teammates before the race began. The race ended up getting delayed for 30 minutes, which goofed me up on my preparedness for the race.

When the race began, I started on the 40 km time trial. Within the first five miles, I passed a rider who had started a minute ahead of me. I kept going at a pace I thought I could maintain for the entire distance. I made it to the turnaround and started back; my body started to 'whine.' I told it to "shut up!" and kept going. I made it to the downhill portion, and then I saw the final big right-hand turn in front of me that took me onto the road that led to the finish. As I was halfway through the turn, another rider came in on the inside of me to my right. He almost hit me. I was frustrated, and it took me a little bit to get settled down. I started to gain on him. As we approached the four-way intersection, a race volunteer was standing in the middle of the road. She had a flag under her arm, and it was pointing right. The guy that almost hit me turned to his right onto that street. I had to follow him, or I would have hit him. Soon as I turned, I knew it was wrong. I stopped quickly and turned around and got back on the course. I proceeded to the finish line.

After cooling down and cleaning up, I loaded my bike and waited for the results to post. I found out that I had taken 3rd place in the male stock bike class. I was frustrated because it looked like my 'forced' mistake cost me a silver medal in that race. My time was 1 hour, 7.02 minutes. I just received a gag gift because neither USA Cycling nor the Minnesota Cycling Federation recognized the stock bike class as a legal class anymore. So, I went and bought myself a bronze medal for cycling. My time wasn't one of my best times for that course, but it was what I got.

*

I woke up one summer day in 2014 with extreme eye pain. I called the Sanford Eye Clinic in Bemidji, MN. They told me to come in right away. My dad and I headed there, and they were able to check my eyes right away. Three different doctors examined me. The last doctor to see me was Dr. Dwyer, who I still go to today.

They discovered that I had glaucoma in my left eye. They sent me to Fargo to see a Dr. Anderson, and he scheduled glaucoma surgery. That surgery was easy compared to others I had endured. A few months later, I was back in Fargo so that Dr. Anderson could do cataract surgery on my left eye.

In 2015 I saw a Dr. Page at the University of Minnesota Eye Clinic because Dr. Dwyer noticed that my right cornea was getting bad. Dr. Page was a cornea specialist. He scheduled a cornea transplant for me.

For this surgery, I had my cousin, Wendy Lundin Kingbay, take me to the hospital. After that surgery, the pressure in that eye was getting too high. Dr. Dwyer told me to come back the next day to see Dr. Ashley Lundin on an emergency basis. My pressure was still high, so she contacted Dr. Anderson in Fargo, and I saw him later that same day. I found out that I had glaucoma in my right eye now. The following week I had glaucoma surgery on the right eye as well.

When they found more cataracts, they sent me to Dr. Page at the university because he knew where the glaucoma tubes were located. The surgery went well, but when I had my next checkup with Dr. Dwyer, he found an issue with my right retina. So, he sent me to yet another doctor—a Dr. Sundeep Dev in St. Cloud. Dr. Dev told me that I had drainage inflammation on my left retina. He gave me an injection in that eye. It went okay, but after my first visit with Dr. Dev, my dad and I left to go to my dad's winter place in Weslaco, Texas. Dr. Dev set me up with another retina doctor down there. When I went to see her, she wasn't going to give me another injection until I told her that I could see rather well before this issue started. She finally gave me the injection.

I got very angry with her when she finished the injection. She bent down and asked me if "we were friends" in a tone of voice that let me know she thought since I had severe disabilities in my hands and other parts of my body, she had assumed that I was mentally disabled as well. The next time I went to see her, I let her know that I had two college degrees and was an elite cyclist. The next time I went to that clinic, I got a different doctor who treated me the same way. I told my Texas glaucoma doctor about how they were treating me at that clinic, and he set me up with a retina doctor that he knew who wouldn't treat me that way.

Now I have good doctors in both Minnesota and Texas. It pays to speak up for yourself. I still get injections in my left eye to this day, but the conditions are stable and not getting worse.

At home on the shores of the Tamarack River in Waskish,
MN 2019

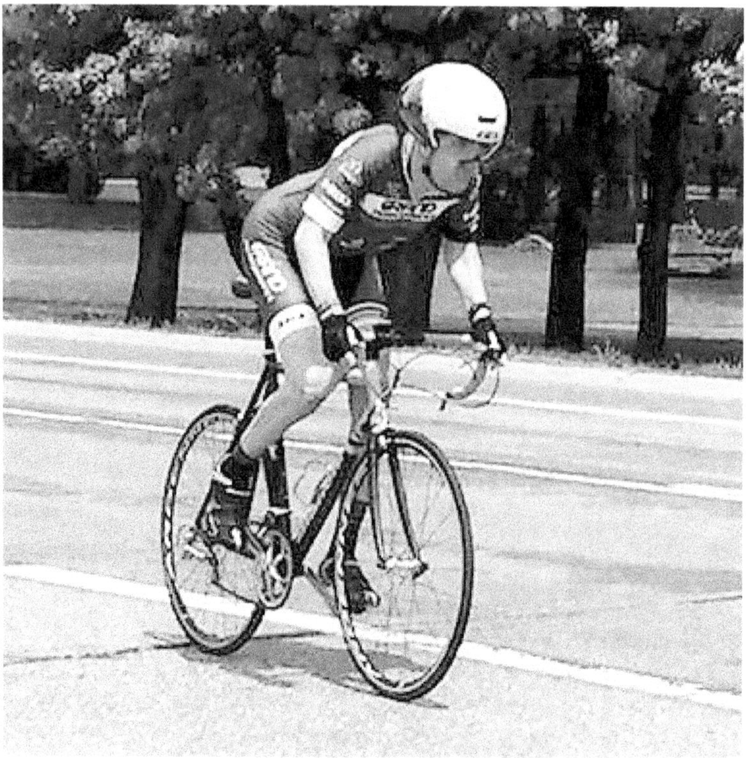

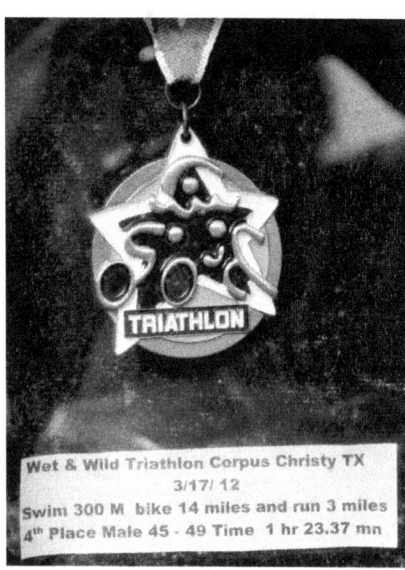

TRIATHLON
Wet & Wild Triathlon Corpus Christy TX
3/17/ 12
Swim 300 M bike 14 miles and run 3 miles
4th Place Male 45 - 49 Time 1 hr 23.37 mn

My Biggest Buck - a 9-Pointer

16

A New Nemesis

In May of 2016, Dad and I headed to St. Cloud to compete in my first Minnesota Senior Olympic games. I was excited because my Olympic dream was about to come true. I have had this dream since 1984. In 1984, I saw two American female cyclists take gold and silver in the first women's Olympic cycling road race.

I was also nervous because I had no idea what shape my body was in. I had no idea what to expect since I was a newcomer to this race. I had a feeling that I'd be the only one competing that had severe disabilities. There was so much going through my mind. On a positive note, I knew I was a good time trialist.

Dad and I made it to St. Cloud fine and got checked into the hotel. Unfortunately, I had to do my pre-race day warmups on the hotel trainer because the road by our hotel did not look safe. I didn't want to overexert myself and injure something. I loaded up on carbs that evening.

The morning of the race, my nerves weren't as bad as I expected them to be. We had breakfast and drove to find the starting place for the 5km and the 10km time trials., Once we knew where we were to go, we went back to the room to wait for a couple of hours.

When we got to the race, my friend, Benita Grams Warns, found me and showed me where the start times were posted; she also filled me in on what to expect that day. My cousin, Kara Lundin, arrived to cheer for me. I headed out to start warming up. When I got back, I found more people came to cheer me on. My cousins Wendy Lundin Kingbay and Stephanie Lundin Kemp were there along with Stephanie's boyfriend, Mike Cooper. I was feeling good and much calmer than I was earlier.

While at the prerace meeting, they informed us that only one-legged starts would be allowed because there were all classes of riders there. It was finally time to start the 10km. I was going to be starting 3rd of 4 riders. I looked at the two in front and thought, "maybe," then I looked at my teammate right behind me. Then I thought, "Oh well, second place is still good."

The buzzer sounded, and I took off. I had a lot of trouble getting my left foot clipped into my peddle. My cousins got nervous, but Dad assured them that I would be fine. I felt good, and it was not long, and my teammate passed me. But when he did, I had the rider that started right in front at 30 seconds in my sight. I passed him just before the turnaround. I reached the turn-around feeling good. Then I had a tailwind to the finish. I crossed the line and was glad that the 10km was done.

After the race, one of the volunteers approached me and introduced himself. It was Mr. Bob Erickson. We had met a few years earlier over the internet. Bob asked me to write a few hunting stories for two of the books that he had published.

When the results for the 10km were posted, I found out that I took 2nd place with a time of 16.32 minutes. I was happy. I had qualified for the 2017 National Senior Games. My cousins knew I was hoping that I could have them put the medal around my neck, but Bob Erickson was giving out the silver medals, as it turned out. When they said my name, Bob had tears in his eyes and was happy to place the award on my neck. I knew I had made his day. They had a guy there taking pictures, and he took one of me with my medal.

When the time came for the 5km, they moved the race to the 10km course instead of the original course and only the first half. My start was rough again because I couldn't get my left foot into the pedal once again and had a headwind for the whole race. I know I passed one rider who had started ahead of me, maybe two. When I got back, I was tired, but I felt good. I ended up retaking 2nd place. My time for the 5km was 9.06 minutes. Again, Bob Erickson was happy to place the silver around my neck. I was feeling great, and I was pleased with my results and how I performed.

*

In the summer of 2016, I was hit with a new nemesis. Real early one summer morning, I woke up very dizzy. I grabbed my cane which I had gotten when I had my broken hip repaired and used that to navigate around my house. I called my doctor, and she said that it sounded like I had vertigo. The staff advised me that I should not travel. That news was hard to accept because I had plans to go to St. Peter, MN, that day to compete in the Minnesota State Time Trial Championships.

I had a cousin who owns a small local paper who wanted to do a story on me and wanted to meet me at the county fair. I was advised not even to go those 30 miles. So, I stayed home.

My cousin Stephanie and her boyfriend, Mike, had come up north to their parent's cabin, so Mike came over and helped me get my new Ipad set up.

This attack was just the first vertigo attack I had. Now I get attacks several times a year over the past five years. Somedays, they are mild, and other days, they are severe. The severe ones hit me hard to the point it makes me get violently sick to my stomach. But even on the days of my not so severe cases, I still try and get a training session on my trainer. But I give myself a day off when they hit hard. When I know that I'm getting a vertigo spell, I get one of my doctor's pills and sit on the trainer if I can. That way, I can work on my therapy exercises while the room is spinning.

In the fall of 2016, I was seeing a pain doctor for my left piriformis issue. (The piriformis is a muscle in the buttocks near the top of the hip joint.) It had been giving me excruciating pain. I also told him about my back pain and the stomach issues I was dealing with. He wanted to try freezing my back. He said that it should help the back pain, plus it might help with the dry heaves I was getting. I had issues with that every day. The dry heaves made training hard. I would get two to four of them when I got out of bed and then after I had breakfast. I would lose my breakfast. I would still force myself onto the trainer but found it hard to train on an empty stomach. My pain doctor froze my back. I had immediate relief from both the severe pain and the dry heaves. I need to have my back refroze every two years.

Also, in the summer of 2016, I was scheduled to have cataract surgery on my right eye. I had an appointment to have it done at the University of Minnesota with Dr. Michael Page, who did the cornea transplant in that eye in 2015. I needed a pre-op exam, so I called my local doctor's office in Kelliher and made an appointment. The appointment went fine, but they decided to give me an EKG, which was no problem, at least I thought anyway. Afterward, I went home, and the CPN called me the next day and told me that she would not be able to give the okay for my surgery. I was shocked and asked her why. She told me that a heart doctor saw something on my EKG.

I was surprised and frustrated because my eye surgery was scheduled. I didn't think I had any problems with my heart.

I called the clinic back and told them that I was just going to have cataracts removed and that I'd be awake during the procedure. The CPN contacted the heart doctor, and he said that if the surgeon doing the cataract surgery was okay with it, he would okay it. They said it would not be a problem, so I was able to get my cataracts removed.

In the meantime, while I was waiting for the surgery, I went to see Dr. Matthew G. Whitbeck, and he didn't tell me what they exactly saw on my EKG, but he said to me that I could just die suddenly without warning and needed to have more tests done. He wanted me to have a nuclear stress test and an echo scan done on my heart and wear a heart monitor.

When I got home, I called the Sanford Hospital in Bemidji and talked with a nurse there. I asked her what size needle they would use for the IV for the nuclear stress test, and she told me a size 22. I told her that I needed a 24 butterfly. She said that it was too small. So, I told her to just do a stress test with me on a bike and forget the IV. She said they couldn't do that because something could happen.

My dad just got back from the post office, and he told me that our postmaster and her husband see a Dr. Watkins in the Sanford Heart Clinic in Bemidji. I decided to give his office a call and make an appointment with him. I also made the appointments for the echo for my heart and set up a heart monitor.

I went in for the echo test and to get a heart monitor. When they put me in a room to get the heart monitor, two young nurses asked if they could watch. I told them it wasn't a problem, that I was glad to help them learn if I could. They asked my nurse what my diagnosis was, and she told them in some medical terms. I asked my nurse if she could speak in 'English' so I could know what was wrong with me, too. She told me that I had a low pulse rate. I told her that my pulse usually is low in the 40 and 50 beats per minute. Then she asked me why I was there. I told her that I was wondering that same question myself.

I only wore the monitor for a week. I called the tech from the company and told her that I was taking it off, and she said that a week was long enough.

When I went in to see Dr. Watkins, they took my dad and me into the room. The doctor asked me why I was there. I told him that I wanted to know what was going on and that I was scared that I might have a severe condition. I told him that I was afraid to stray too far from home. I didn't want to be back on a gravel forestry road on my bike, and something happens to me. There was hardly any traffic on those roads I road and no one would find me. He said, "Mr. Stillar, this whole thing was blown way out of proportion." He told me that since I train as I do, it was typical for me to have a low resting heart rate. He told me just to keep doing what I was doing, and there was no threat to my heart.

That is one reason I train as I do. My dad's brothers and sisters and my mother's dad and family all had heart problems, and I want to keep my heart strong.

*

Wednesday, May 17, 2017, I washed my Bianchi San Lorenzo for the 2017 Minnesota Senior Games. I was wiping down the tip tube when the rear Brazz-on for the rear brake cable broke off. I panicked a little and grabbed two zip ties and fastened it up. I emailed my friend, the owner of Grand Performance Bike Shop in St. Paul. I told him what happened, and he told me to take pictures and email them to him. After he saw them, he advised me not to race the bike now. I didn't panic because I had my Croll with me. (That a guy built for me in 1999.)

I went and put my good racing wheels on the Croll, but the gear shifting was way off. So, I called Grand Performance back and asked if one of the mechanics had time to fix my bike the next day. She told me to bring it on in. My dad and I headed to the Cities the next day. They were able to get to fixing it right away. Dad and I went to get a bite to eat, and when we got back to the shop, it was almost ready. They checked everything over and said it was 'good to go.'

Dad and I headed to Mankato. After breakfast the following day, we headed out to find the location of the race. We found it and then headed back to the hotel to have lunch. I then got sick because of my hiatal hernia. But I brushed that off and headed out to the Time Trials.

When I unloaded my bike, a rider stopped by our car and told me that he almost crashed on the bridge after the hill at 35 mph. He said it was too dangerous to race on that bridge. I got my bike ready, got my chip, and headed out to do my warm-up.

I made it to the 5km turn around and saw the hill ahead. I decided to try it. I had to ride my brakes down the hill and stayed at 20 mph. The rider was right; that course was too dangerous. I couldn't complain because my Croll was just a standard road racing bike and not a time-trial bike.

After the race director started hearing concerns about that hill, he decided to run the race himself. He returned and informed us that he would be choosing a different and safer course, but it would delay the start by thirty minutes. He would let those of us who were there test the new route. I went out with another guy and found out that there were no hills to contend with this time. I felt much better about the course, and that I could drop the other guy I went out with halfway through was even better.

The first division was the 50 – 54 age group for males, so I had to line up first. I only saw one rider ahead of me. There were supposed to be three others alongside me, but only one guy rolled up and informed the starter that he wouldn't be doing the 10km time trial. I knew then that I had the silver. I was going to do my best even if I didn't have any competition.

I had a little problem getting my left foot clipped into the pedal, but it wasn't as bad as in 2016. I started good and felt good. About halfway through the course, a teammate of mine, Rick Christenson, passed me, but he was in the male age bracket of 55 – 59, and he was on a time trial bike. I finished the course feeling good about my ride. When I got back to the car, Dad said that my teammate won and came in first. I had to correct him and let Dad know that he was in a different age bracket. I asked Dad how far I was behind him, and he told me it wasn't long. That encouraged me.

When they posted the results, I saw my name in the first-place spot. It didn't sink in right away. The rider who had dropped out earlier pointed out that I had taken the gold in that time trial. My teammate, Rick, also pointed out that I came in 3rd overall among 22 riders. He told me that he thought that was awesome since I was on a Croll and not a time trial bike. I had received my first gold medal in the Senior Olympic Time Trial. My time for the 10km was 16.03 minutes.

Soon after, I got ready for the 5km time trial. This time no riders were dropping out in my age bracket. I started last, but I started strong. At the 5km turn around, the race volunteer stepped into my way, and I almost jack-knifed the bike, trying to avoid hitting him and make the turn at the same time. One foot even came out of my clip. Even with that close call, I was able to catch and pass the 4th place rider at the two-mile mark. I knew at that point that I'd be getting a medal. I crossed the line feeling happy with myself. The guy that I passed came up to me and told me that he was frustrated in himself because he let me pull past him, then he saw that it was a rider on a Croll. He told me he was honored that I did beat him.

I received the bronze medal for my age class with a time of 8.10 minutes. There was 24 riders total, and I took 5th overall - not bad for this Apert Syndrome guy.

My Gold Medal from the MN Senior Games in Mankato, MN

17

A Golden Mistake

It was April of 2018, and my dad got himself a 'lady friend.' Dad met her in Texas. She had lost her husband about the same time that my mother died. Her name is Melva Worley, and she lives just down the street and around the corner from us in Texas. When Dad and Melva first got together, she and her daughter would come to Minnesota to visit Dad at Waskish, but she hasn't been here for a couple of years.

It didn't really bother me when they got together because Dad assured me that they were just friends. Melva doesn't like to fish and hunt as my mother did, but she loves to dance. She and Dad go dancing often and go to concerts. They also like taking short trips together to see different things. Besides keeping Dad busy while we are in Texas, it gives me a lot more time to myself.

On the 13th of April, Dad, Melva, and I headed up to San Antonio, TX, for the Texas Senior Games. It was going to be my third senior game, but my first one in Texas. I would be competing in the 10km and 5km cycling time trials on Saturday and Sunday.

Once we got to San Antonio, we had a little trouble finding where I was to check in. Then we got lost trying to get to our hotel. We got there a lot later than I had hoped we would. They had a vast sports complex next door to get a little spin on the bike that evening. Then we got lost going to and coming back from dinner.

The following day, we got lost again, trying to get to where the cycling events would be held. Melva finally used her GPS on her phone because the car's GPS just wasn't working for us. We finally got there, and I got registered for the 10km. I was able to get a little warm-up in.

When I got back to the car, Dad told me that my cousin Scott Davies was looking for me. I changed my shoes and headed for the start. I found my cousin, but the rider's meeting was starting, and it was getting close to the beginning of the time trial. The first rider was supposed to begin at 9 am, and it was already 9:30 am. They told us that we were all going to get new start times. When I got my new start time, I found I had a little time to chat with my cousin.

I noticed that they had not changed the start times on the computer screens, and I started to get nervous. I began to worry that I had missed my start time, and I started my warm-up for the ride but stayed close to the starting line. I figured that I had twenty minutes until the start. But as I rode by the starting line, I noticed all the riders were gone. I pulled in, and my dad came and told me that they had called my name, and I didn't show. The race was over. I was upset.

They had given me a new starting time and thought I had twenty minutes left. I went and spoke to an official. I asked him if he could help me. I told him that I had missed my starting time because I was given a different one and wondered why they returned to the original times. He told me that I was right, that new times were set, but the riders just started showing up at the old times, so they let them go. He could see that I was frustrated. He told me to hang on, and he'd go figure this out. Pretty soon, he came back and said to me that they would let me race.

I went and got my bike back on the road and one foot in the pedal. He gave me a quick count down, and I was off. My emotions were so high that I had a hard time getting my breathing under control. Finally, it got better, and I started going down the first hill where the turn was. There was a huge fire truck at the bottom of the hill. As I approached the right-hand lane for the riders, I saw an ambulance right in the middle of the road. I only had about two feet or less to get by it. I had to slow down to make it by safely. Then I made it up the hill and back to the road where the start was.

I started my second full lap and had to slow down for the ambulance again; that is when I noticed a rider down. It looked like he crashed hard. I made it to the finish line and did two small laps to cool down.

When I got back to the start, my cousin asked me how I did. I told him that I didn't do good because I had to slow down so much for that accident. One of the riders told me to punch my number into the computer monitor to see how I did. I punched it in, but I didn't know how to read it. I was sure I had come in last because my time was 16.39 minutes. It was one of my slowest times compared to what I had done in Minnesota. I brushed it off and told my cousin and my dad that I took the last place. We said goodbye to my cousin and headed back to the hotel.

Dad informed me that he and his lady friend would like to leave that day and head back to Weslaco, but I told them "No" because I didn't want to go and miss the 5km the next day. If I saw the times and knew their times, and knew I could have beaten them, I would have been frustrated. I suggested we use Melva's phone in the morning for the GPS so we wouldn't get lost again. I'm not sure if they were happy with me because we ended up going to separate places for dinner that night, within walking distance, so that we wouldn't get lost.

The following day went much better. We used the phone for the GPS and got there in plenty of time. I saw an official, and he told me that today's start times would be honored. They had changed the course to an 'out and back course.' I was able to get in a better warm-up. I didn't want to take the chance of missing the start, so I was there early. I heard a volunteer ask a rider, two in front of me, if he wanted a holding start, he said 'yes.' Then he was off. The rider in front of me didn't want to be held; then, it was my turn. The volunteer asked me if I wanted to be held and said 'yes.' Then I knew today would be better than the day before. They said 'go,' and I went.

As I approached the first corner, I saw that I was catching a rider. Shortly after the corner, I passed him, and I was feeling even better. Then I got another rider in my sights, and after the turnaround, I passed him, too. I had gained a least a minute, if not more, on that rider. As I started up the final hill in the route, I had to get up out of the saddle and use my climbing legs. As I approached the finish, I caught another rider but did not have time to pass him because he got into the finishing chute before me. I slowed down a bit because I did not want to run into him. I crossed the finish line and did a short cool down.

I punched my number into the computer screen this time, and I saw a little number 3 by my name. I asked another rider what that 3 meant, and he told me that I had got third place, the bronze medal. I continued checking the screen until the race was over. I still had that three by my name. I asked when the awards would be and found out that they were to be held right after the 40km. I wasn't doing that race, so I asked if I could get my medal early, and they told me that it would be no problem. When she handed me my bronze medal, she had a gold medal with it. All I knew is that I was receiving a bronze. I told her she made a mistake, and I gave the gold medal back to her.

The following day, I went to their website and saw the times were posted. I checked the 5 km results and found that I had placed third, bronze for the male age 50 – 54 division with 9.26 minutes. There were ten riders in that division. There were 61 riders for the 5km, and I placed 10th overall. Then I looked at Saturday's 10km results, and that is when I got a huge surprise. I found out they didn't make a mistake and gave me someone else's gold medal. In that race, which I thought I had come in last, I found out that I had taken first with my time of 16.39 minutes. There were 6 in my age group with 68 riders, total. I took gold for my age group and 8th place overall.

I printed off the results and showed my dad. He could not believe it. I called the organizers and told them that I did win the gold medal for the male 50 – 54 age group in the 10km. They sent me my medal. This gold was my second gold medal for the Senior Olympics.

*

Back in Minnesota that year, Dad and I got ready to head to the 2018 Minnesota Senior Games – 10km Time Trials in Mankato on August 18th. I had my new carbon fiber Bianchi Aria this year; I was still nervous about the 10km race. I wondered if they still had the same dangerous course as the year before. I was not sure what course they would be using.

Once I got there and picked up my 'welcome bag,' I found out that the 10km course was the same that they had switched to the year before. My confidence returned. We were staying at a better hotel with better restaurants. Now I could choose food that would work better with my hiatal hernia. There were also better roads around the hotel to stretch my legs out after the long drive. I was able to get a great warm-up once we got to Mankato, then went and had a great carbo-loaded meal.

After breakfast the following day, we headed to the starting location. I started my warm-up and was feeling good. This year they did the woman's age groups first.

It was a better start this time. As I approached the first turn, I was catching the rider that had started in front of me. I passed that rider at the halfway mark and started catching up to another rider. I caught up and passed a woman rider who was still out on the course from the races that started six minutes before us. Then a little later, I passed another lady rider shortly after I crossed the finish line.

I took 2nd place out of 6 riders with 15.10 minutes for the 10km race. The next day was the 5km. Again, I had another great warm-up and another good start. It was a good race, and I finished strong. I placed 2nd out of four riders that day with a time of 7.43 minutes. I brought home two silvers. I was happy because I had qualified for the National Senior Games for 2019. I did great for being on a new bike.

*

That fall was the 2018 Minnesota Deer Archery Hunting Season. Dad and I drove out to our stands. He dropped me off at the field, and I got ready, and my crossbow cocked. I grabbed my backpack and walked back into the woods. The woods looked different this year where I walked back to my stand. Many trees had been blown down from strong winds in the summer of 2018; it was either straight-line winds or a mini-tornado that hit some spots.

When I got to my stand, I climbed up, put my bag and seat cushion up in it, and then took my crossbow up. I put the crossbow on the floor and then climbed over the railing and finished getting ready to hunt. It was about 4:50 pm before I was done settling in. Then I waited to see what might come my way that night.

It was about an hour and fifteen minutes, and I had seen nothing. That is when I said, "Oh Mom, it is 6:10 pm. You have 20 minutes to drive a deer to Dad or me." I always talked to my mother, even though she passed away in 2007. I know she is always with me. About fifteen minutes later, I saw some movement in the woods. It was a deer. I kept my eye on it, but it disappeared for a little bit. Then all-of-a-sudden, I saw it within range. I pulled up my crossbow and took the safety off. I aimed and fired. I watched my arrow hit.

I called Dad to let him know that I might have a deer down. I gathered my things and brought them down out of the stand. It was only 6:30 pm. I knew we only had about thirty minutes to find it before it got too dark. I found my arrow. When I saw that, I knew I had hit the deer. I had a little trouble finding the trail. My dad got to my stand, and he started finding signs of the trail, but it was tough to follow, but we finally found the deer.

After we got it ready to drag out to the pickup, it had gotten dark. Dad had a flashlight, and I had my tracking light and a lamp on my head. We had plenty of light to find our way. I had a compass, but Dad didn't have his. That was our first mistake.

We made a little progress on dragging the deer by hand. The woods were thick where we were, so Dad decided to go alone and find the pickup. I checked my compass and gave him bearings to head, but he wanted to try a different direction.

It was not long, and I couldn't hear him anymore nor see his light. More time went by, and still no sight of my dad. I started to holler out to him to see where he was, but I heard nothing from him. That's when I began to worry about my 82-year-old father. Here is where I realized our second mistake. We didn't have our radios or our phones with us. I had no idea where he was. I did not know if he had fallen and gotten hurt or was still on the way. I did think a few times of trying to find the pickup myself, but I knew if I did that, I would have to leave my jacket with the deer. I didn't have the key for the pickup anyway, so I just stayed put.

I started to look around and get a little scared because the only weapon I had with me was my hunting knife, and I knew a dead deer would draw in the coyotes and wolves. Finally, I heard my dad yelling. He found his way back to me. So, then I left my jacket, and we headed out and saw the pickup lights. I put my stuff in the pickup and headed back to the house. Dad told me that he got turned around in the woods. Because of the storm and all the blown-down trees, everything looked different. When he finally found the road, he was a mile away from the pickup. I told him that we made several mistakes that night, and he agreed.

The following day, we went back and made a four-wheeler trail back to where the deer laid next to my jacket. When I got home, I made a list of things we needed to have with us for the 2019 deer season if we get another deer.

First deer with a rifle in 1985

18

Minnesota Determination

After our experiences the year before getting lost in San Antonio so many times, I wasn't sure if Dad would ever go back. I asked my dad if I could go to the Texas Senior Games again in 2019. He agreed to go back. We found a hotel closer to the race site with a restaurant with food I could eat.

I contacted Aunt Maxine and Uncle Chuck and told them that we would do the games again. I also got a hold of my cousin Scott Davies and let him know we wanted to see his parents.

Dad and I headed up to San Antonio on March 30, 2019. We met had arranged to meet my aunt and uncle at a restaurant when we got there, but something came up, and they couldn't make it, but the food was good. We made our way over to pick up my "Welcome Bag" and t-shirt and then headed to our hotel. After we checked in, I got ready and went out for a ride. This time I found some excellent roads with bike lanes to ride that was close to the hotel.

After breakfast the following day, I put the race site into the GPS, and we had no problem getting there that year. I met with an official, and he assured me that everything would be on time and filled me in on the new 10km course. It was only 47 degrees F out that day. It was cool. I just had my team skin suit on with just arm warmers and an athletic tank top underneath. My teammate, Dan Casebeer, and my cousin Jeremy Sartain advised me on how to dress for it.

I realized that my bike had a mechanical issue in the shifting, so I had to wait until the bike mechanic got there. He finally showed, and luckily my start time for the 5km was at the end of the field. I had time for the mechanic to look at my bike and get the shifting adjusted for me. I did a little more warming up, and then it was off to the start.

The volunteer at the start asked me if I wanted a holding start; I told him that I did—that gave me the chance to get both of my feet clipped into the pedals. When the starter said, "Go!" I took off. I quickly got into a rhythm. It wasn't long, and I was at the turn-around point. The return, back to the finish, went great. When I got done, I did a cooldown, got a snack and a protein shake out of the cooler, and got into the car to warm up. I didn't have too long to rest because the 10km was soon to start.

I rode up the road that was a mile or two behind the 5km start line. The 10km time trial had a different course than the year before. It was better, and I felt good about it. This course had about a quarter to half a mile uphill start. Other than that, it was the same course as the 5km except for the added distance. I thought I was the last one on the course because I was the only one in the male 50 – 54 age group, unlike in the 5km where I had to chase two other riders. This time there was no one to hold the riders, but I was okay with that. I have done quite a few one-legged starts.

Soon it was my turn, and the starter said, "Go!" I blasted up the road and quickly got into a rhythm. I flew up the hill and headed to the finish. After the finish, I did another cooldown. Then I got another protein shake in me and headed up to the pavilion, where the results would be announced. I saw the one volunteer I knew. He told me that it would be another twenty minutes, so I went back to the car and got my dad.

When we got back, other cyclists saw that I was still wearing my skinsuit with just arm warmers, and my legs were bare. They all asked me if I was crazy. I then asked them if telling them that I was only a winter Texan from Minnesota, that I was born and raised in International Falls, the Ice Box of the Nation, and that the wind chill can be 50 or 60 below in the winter - if that would make a difference in how they viewed me? They said, "For sure!" They told me they thought I was incredible.

They started handing out the medals for both the 5km and 10km time trials. I came back with a gold medal in each for my age group. My time for the 5km was 8.07 minutes, and for the 10km, it was 16.14 minutes. My last two times in the Texas Senior Games, I won three golds and one bronze.

It was windy that day. On the morning of April 10th of 2019, I woke up at my dad's mobile home in Texas, planning to go out riding. Because of the wind, I decided to change my route and just do a few laps around the city of Weslaco. It was just after 9 in the morning when I left my dad's park. I made it up to 6th Street onto Texas Boulevard, then back down to 18th Street. I turned right on 18th, and when I got to Border Avenue, I decided to take a right and take Border back up to 6th Street. There was a slight rise there that went over a water dike. All I remember is that I made it over the dike.

The next thing I knew, I was looking at the First Responders or Paramedics who were putting me on a backboard and placing a neck collar on me. They loaded me into an ambulance and took me to the Knapp Medical Center in Weslaco.

When I got to the hospital, I was more aware of what was going on but still had no idea what had happened. Someone asked if they could call someone for me. I told them, "Yes," that they needed to call my dad. They tried, but dad was not inside his mobile home and didn't answer. I told him to call the staff at the park my dad was in, Country Sunshine, and have them get a message to him.

The nurse came into the room I was in and told me that they needed to put an IV in. I told her that she needed a 24-butterfly needle to do the IV and showed her the spot where she needed to put it in. She said they only had a regular 22 size needle. I let her know that they wouldn't get it in with that, but she was determined to use it.

By then, my dad had arrived and was getting angry with the nurse. He knew she was putting me into more pain than I was already in by trying to use the size 22 needle. She couldn't get the IV in my arm. She gave up and sent me to x-ray. They found out that my right pelvis was broke in two places. The doctor was frustrated because I did not have an IV in yet. He wanted to have a scan done of my pelvic to see if there was any bleeding. If there was, I would have to have surgery. A younger nurse decided to call Imaging to see if a 24-butterfly needle would work. They told her it would, and they finally got the IV in.

They did the scan and found out that it was a clean break and there was no bleeding. I didn't need to go to surgery. About four hours later, they got me into a room. My first nurse was great, but I did not like the night shift nurse. First, he said that the doctor ordered heavy pain medication for me. I told him that I did not want it. He kept insisting on it. I finally gave in and said, "Okay," but only if they got me something to eat so it wouldn't upset my stomach. But they just brought me the pain medication.

I tried to sleep but didn't get much of that. A lady from the cafeteria woke me up by bringing me a tuna fish sandwich at 2:30 in the morning. I asked her what that was. She told me that is what I ordered. I said, "Mam, I did not order anything like this; I wanted something five and a half hours earlier to go with the pain medication so it wouldn't upset my stomach, not at 2:30 in the morning." But I ate it anyway, but I wasn't happy. Then another nurse came in at 3 am and told me she would change my bedding and give me a bath. I told her that this was crazy and that this type of thing does not happen in Minnesota at three in the morning, maybe at six, but not at three.

Then at 6:30 in the morning, they brought me breakfast, and it wasn't at all what I had ordered the night before. Then my nurse and orthopedic doctor (from the clinic I go to) came into my room. Finally, I felt like I was going to be treated with some respect from them. My orthopedic doctor ordered physical therapy for me.

The second night, just before I went to bed, an imaging tech came into my room. He said that he had orders to do a scan of the arteries in my neck. I told him that I couldn't understand why they wanted a scan of my neck. That is when they informed me that it was probable that I had been hit by a car, that I didn't just fall off my bike. I did not know what happened to me, but I figured I must have gotten hit by a car because of my broken pelvis. He had his orders, so they did the scan and couldn't find anything wrong with my neck.

The night nurse got upset with my day nurse because she had disconnected my IV from the bag. I told him that I was eating solid food and drinking liquid. A few hours later, the orthopedic doctor's assistant came in and said to me that they were releasing me from the hospital the following day.

Dad went to the pharmacist to get my medications. The pharmacy owner figured out it was my dad, and he handed him a piece of paper with a name on it. He told my dad that the lady on the paper saw the accident or something concerning it. That's when I called the police department. An officer came to my dad's home. The officer contacted the witness, but she told him that I was already on the ground when she saw me.

I called the police department to see if I could get a copy of the police report. They told me to contact records at the city hall. I called and sent that lady the information. I then received the police report. I got angry when I read it. It said that the First Responders had responded to an elderly gentleman who had fallen from his bike. It also had it worded that made me aware that the first responders, the police officers, and the Knapp Medical Center had assumed that I was also mentally handicapped. I can't prove it for sure, but after living with this syndrome for over 50 years, you can tell what people actually mean when they say certain things.

*

It was now August 1st, 2019. Dad and I had come home to Northern Minnesota and were heading to St. Cloud so I could compete in the 2019 Minnesota Senior Olympics. I was going to compete in the 5km and the 10km time trials.

Sixteen weeks before this, I was laying on the road in Weslaco, Texas, a victim of an assumed hit and run with a broken pelvis. But I couldn't let that deter my dreams. Two weeks afterward, I was spinning on the floor exerciser. By the end of May, I rode the trainer and outside on my bike for short rides. I had no idea what my actual condition was for racing since I had not been pushing it in my training yet.

Dad and I got to St. Cloud and got checked in at the race and then checked into our hotel. That evening I rode a recon of the course, but I already knew it; I just wanted to ensure there weren't any bad spots in the road that appeared since I was there last. I was ready for the next day. My body felt good, and I was feeling good about my chances.

The next morning, Dad and I headed for the start area. That is where I met a new friend. His name is Marcel Derosier, and he was going to be racing in my age division. We talked, and I filled him in on the course since it was his first time there.

After my warm-up, my cousins Wendy Lundin Kingbay and Kara Lundin arrived. I went to pick up my electronic chip; while I was waiting, another friend, David Peterson, walked up. He rolled his eyes and said, "Aww, great, YOU showed up." I knew he was just funning with me. I told him not to worry about me because I was still recovering from a broken pelvis, and I filled him in on what happened to me. When I got back to the car, I saw that another friend showed up, Bob Erickson from St. Cloud. He was the friend who had me write a couple of hunting stories for his book a few years before. He told me that he was confident for a win for me, but I told him about my accident and that I was just recovering from a broken pelvis, so I wasn't sure what the day would bring.

When it was time for the 5km to start, David, Marcel, and the few others in line started giving me a hard time. But I gave it right back to them. I had a better start than I did three years ago. I quickly got into a rhythm and was feeling good. I got a little frustrated at the turnaround, but I only went a few feet more. I started heading back. I looked down at my heart rate, and it was 171 bpm. I crossed the finish line and was happy, though I did not know how I did. They held the awards shortly afterward, and I found out that I took 2nd place out of the five riders in my age division, bringing home the silver medal. My friend Marcel took the gold, and David took the bronze. I had averaged 23.08 mph, and my time was 8.07 minutes.

I felt my body was at its limit this time around, even though I had a great start in the 10km. The other two riders in my age division were Randall Giles and Bruce Truebenbach. One of them came up to me after the race to tell me that I had a good race and that he was afraid that I would pass him. I told him that I had only passed one rider but was gaining on another two riders at the finish. When the group of us was waiting for the 10km awards, they asked me how

I had broken my pelvis. I told them about the assumed hit and run in Texas in April. They were shocked that I was back to racing only 16 weeks after being in the hospital. They were amazed and told me that they thought that I was incredible to do what I did in the time trials.

When it was time for the awards, I found out that I took 2nd place, a silver medal once again. My time for the 10km was 16.14 minutes at an average speed of 22 to 30 mph. I was on cloud nine; despite my rough year, I was going home with two silver medals.

*

For the last several years, I have been primarily archery deer hunting with my crossbow. I don't trophy hunt. I just hunt for food to feed Dad and me. My grandpa Max had shared stories with me about what he had to do for his family when he was young, and I wanted to follow in his footsteps.

I was out in my deer stand in the fall of 2019 Archery Season. Dad and I knew a storm might be coming in later that evening but thought we could get the evening hunt in before it hit.

I got situated in my stand, but the hunt did not last long. The storm started to move in. It was a bit after 6 pm, and I heard my dad coming to pick me up. When he stopped the pickup, he honked the horn. I started to get my stuff gathered up and into my backpack to get ready to leave. I put my crossbow on the floor of the stand, climbed over the railing to start to crawl down. I got both my feet on the top rung of the ladder. Then the top railing, which I was holding on to, let loose. I fell eight feet to the ground but ended up landing on both feet. I landed like a paratrooper. Soon as I hit, I went to my knees. Then I fell forward and hit my head on the ladder. It didn't knock me out so, I got up and checked my head and figured it was fine.

I checked my right foot because that hit the ladder's bottom rung on the way down. It was sore, but it didn't feel broken. I climbed back up into the stand and got my backpack and seat cushion down. Then I went back up and got my crossbow. I walked the 50 yards to the pickup. My toes were a little black the next day, but that lasted only a few days, and then it was back to training.

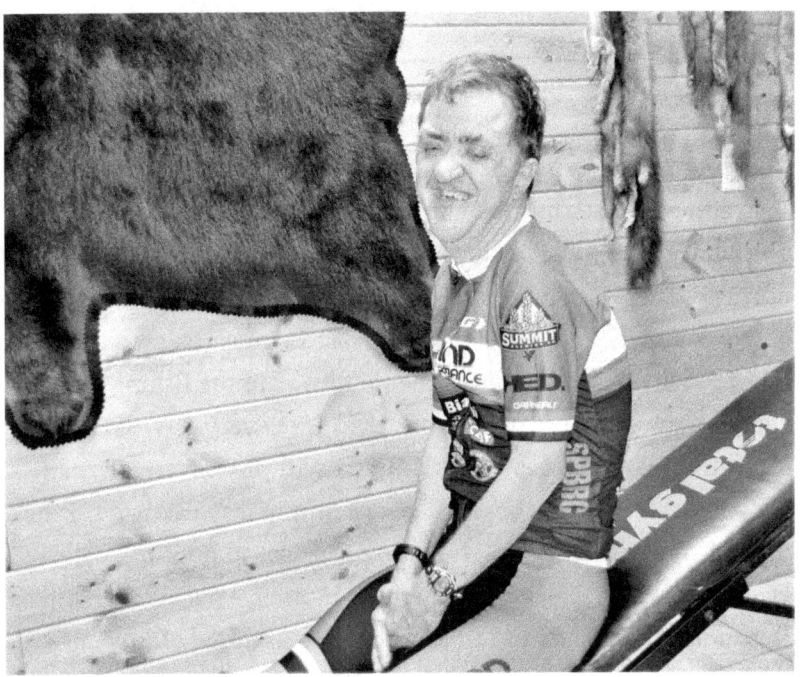

Visiting with my cousin Rena, (who took the photo) in my training room in Waskish. Notice my bearskin on the wall.

19

My Dad

I owe my dad a lot. I am sure he wanted a completely normal son rather than settling for a son who had a rare syndrome and had special needs. But luckily for me, both Dad and Mom treated me as normally as they could.

Now understand, I don't remember too much from when I was little, but my parents had told me that I was in the fishing boat and enjoying the outdoors with them when I was very tiny. To me, that is treating me like a normal kid. Even with my severe disabilities, my parents took me grouse and deer hunting. My dad had this motorized trail bike that we would use for grouse hunting, or it was Dad and me in the pickup. Sometimes mother would come with us. When it came to deer hunting, both Mom and Dad hunted deer.

When my dad was in school, he played sports – football and basketball. When I got old enough, my dad put up a basketball hoop. We would play one on one games. Dad would just let me do it the best I could. He didn't care if I dribbled or not.

Dad was also a great fast-pitch softball pitcher. He made sure I always had a bat and a ball, even though the ball was usually a tennis ball. Dad would pitch under-handed and gently to me. He played on a softball team in International Falls when I was young. His teammates always treated me with respect. On game days, I got to play with his other teammate's children.

I didn't see my dad much in the summertime because he worked for the county in the engineering department. He designed and built roads and bridges. On several occasions, he would stop by the house and pick me up. I would go with him to wherever the job took him that day. But mostly, my dad would be gone off to work before I even woke up in the morning.

On weekends, my parents and I would either go camping and fishing or see grandparents, aunts, and uncles. Our family was close, and we did almost everything together.

Dad taught me how to hunt, and he even taught me how to trap animals for fur. That was something my dad did when he was young to make money. So, instead of staying inside and playing video games like the kids do today, I was either out walking in the swamps or driving (after I was old enough to get my license) to check my traplines.

When I landed the job as a production assistant at a television station in Duluth, I only saw my parents every other weekend. It was that way for a long time. I would try to get home to see my parents as often as I could.

In December of 2004, I moved back home with my parents. I had just had my right shoulder replaced and found out that I couldn't work anymore in that field of work. I feel that it was all in the plan that the "man upstairs" had for me. A year and a half later, my mother was diagnosed with stage 4 terminal esophageal cancer. At the same time, my left shoulder gave out. I also felt that I was needed at home, and I wanted to spend that time with my mother.

When my mother passed away, Dad's and my relationship changed in a way. He started to depend on me more to help with certain things. Dad took care of the gardens, but I began to take over the lawn mowing for a time. Now, Dad took over the lawn mowing again, and I took over the cooking. Dad has told me that I am a better cook than he is. I don't use a recipe book. I just make whatever comes off my head, whatever sounds good at the time. I take care of the technical things, like the TV and the internet. I am responsible for making all the calls to keep connected with both when we travel from Minnesota to Texas and back again.

After my mother's death, things started to change for me in Texas. At first, it was gradual changes. In 2005 I started doing park rides in their retirement community with my parents and their friends. After my mother died, I also started riding with my friends who were my age. Doing both rides was taxing on my body, so I had to cut one out. I decided to stick with the riders more my age. We would do 25 – 50-mile rides.

Over a year to two years after my mom passed, Dad began seeing a lady friend. I was happy for him because now he had someone to be with when we are in Texas, plus now he had someone who liked to dance as much as he did. I'm alone a lot more than I used to be, but that is okay.

Even though I would rather stay in Minnesota year-round, I know I need to stick with my dad because we need each other. Dad can't take Minnesota's cold winters anymore. He needs me here too. I was becoming a caretaker for my dad now. In February of 2019, Dad suffered two strokes. Luckily, they did not affect him too badly, and he was back to normal in a few months. He has had other medical issues as well. Now I'm the one reminding him to take his medications every night.

I was born with the deck stacked against me, but I hope you will now know that I did not let it stop me with the stories I shared in this book. I had over 30 surgeries in my lifetime, with three of them being very risky. But I made it through them. I want to thank my dad, Patrick Stillar, and my late mother, Jacque Stillar, for providing their special needs child a "normal" life. Also, for letting me chase my dreams. I also want to thank my aunts, uncles, cousins, grandparents, friends, and teammates for their support.

Some people may wonder why I train so hard since I have not worked since 2004. The reason is that several of my doctors and my physical therapist have encouraged me to keep training. They told me that I didn't keep training and that my body would eventually worsen, and I'd have more problems to deal with in my life.

I train six days a week because I do not know what Apert Syndrome has in store for me next. Along with Apert, there are other things to consider. Heart problems, diabetes, and high blood pressure all ran in my family members. So, I am determined to give this syndrome and my family health history a formidable foe.

As I write this, in the year 2020, the COVID-19 virus is changing the world, and people live in fear of getting sick. With the condition of my body, getting COVID-19 would be hard on me. Though I am afraid of getting sick, I know that I am better off than most people. I am unsure what it would do to my body with its physical deformities, both external and internal. I know it would hit me hard.

It frustrates me that the governments of this world did not do more right away to stop this virus. I worry about my brothers and sisters worldwide who have Apert Syndrome, because many have a worse case than I do.

Dealing with this virus has distracted me and has made it harder for me to achieve my cycling dreams. This situation has added additional stress. Not only do I worry about getting the virus myself, but I worry about my 85-year-old dad getting sick. All I can do is focus on getting my training every day and staying safe as possible from this virus. I have reached many dreams and goals in my life, but I have many more to achieve and fulfill.

My Dad - Patrick Stillar

Patrick Stillar - Stationed in Germany in the 1950's

20

What's Next

It is March 8th, 2021, and I am sitting in my dad's mobile home in the retirement park in Weslaco, Texas. So far, Dad and I have survived this Covid-19 pandemic. Dad got his first vaccine shot last Friday. I haven't gotten mine yet, because all the pharmacy appointments are taken. If I need to wait until I get back home to Minnesota seven weeks from now, I will wait. I know my immune support system is strong. I will just wait to see what happens.

This winter of 2020 and 2021 has been rough here in South Texas, simply because the virus has been bad here all winter. I have been staying inside except for making runs and going to appointments. Then all our electricity was out for several days during an unusual cold snap, and Dad and I had to sleep in the living room wearing our "Minnesota" winter gear.

I have mainly ridden on my trainer in my dad's "Texas" room because I have not wanted to venture outside. In part because of the pandemic, the hit and run that happened to me in 2019 is always on my mind. I don't want anything to happen that would require a trip to the emergency room. I remember how I was treated at that hospital, and I don't want to return.

Just last week, another hit and run happened close to the same spot that mine occurred. The police are looking for the driver this time. The local news reports it as a hit and run, where my "hit and run" was broadcast as "an elderly gentleman fallen from his bicycle." That still frustrates me a lot.

I'm going to use that frustration to motivate me in my training. Right now, I only have two Senior Olympic Games on my calendar. The first one is the Minnesota Senior Games in Mankato in August and the South Dakota Senior Games in September. I am planning on some small weeknight-time trial series in the Twin Cities area. Plus, I am hoping the Minnesota State Cycling Time Trial Championships will be held again. I want to see if I can get my sixth gold medal. But I'll take any color medal as long as it's the best I can do that day.

The USA Cycling Masters Time Trial Championships this coming year is part of my plan, but so far, they haven't got them scheduled yet. Covid has changed so many things in our world. I will compete in them whenever they get scheduled. I was qualified to compete in this year's National Senior Games in Fort Lauderdale, Florida, in June. But due to covid, they got postponed to May 2022. If they decide to schedule any of these on the days of the Minnesota Fishing Opener, I will be staying home and going fishing. I need to set my priorities. That is the weekend I get to see some of my uncles and cousins that I haven't seen in six months.

I plan to do several national senior games in the years to come if I qualify for them. I don't think qualifying will be a problem because I have no plans on stopping my training anytime soon.

I'd like to do some "world" senior games. I'm not sure if there are such events or not. I know that there are the Huntsman World Senior Games in St. George, Utah, every year. I hope to be participating in that in the future. I want to participate in the World Senior Games that include athletes from Eastern European Countries.

There is a family here in the United States who have adopted a young baby boy with Apert from an Eastern Bloc Country. I want to race against athletes from countries that might not understand children with disabilities nor treat them well. I want to show the people that everyone should be treated equally, regardless of if they are able-bodied or disabled or what their nationality or religion is.

When I compete in the United States National Senior Games, I will be fulfilling a promise that I made to myself years ago. My Great Uncle Lyle passed away several years ago. I remember him as an excellent archer with a bow and arrow. He had qualified for the National Senior Games one year, but unfortunately, he did not get to go because he had some heart issues that prevented him from going. When I heard the news, I was saddened. I made myself a promise that one day I would go and compete in the National Senior Games in the cycling time trials. That is a huge challenge for me, but I have competed in the Minnesota Senior Games four times and the Texas Senior Games twice, and between them, I have four gold medals, four silver medals, and two bronze medals, and even though I will be up against athletes with no disabilities, I know that I can get on the podium on one of those steps in the nationals. I believe in myself, and I have the support I need from my family, friends, and teammates.

My dad will turn 85 this year on St. Patrick's Day, which is just a few days away. Dad is still in good condition for his age, especially compared to the other seniors in his retirement park in Texas. I figure he has a few good years left. I will be making the trip down to South Texas with him until we can't go anymore. I am the only person that can legally make decisions for him if he can't make them for himself.

I don't like it in Texas because the roads are not good for biking, plus the drivers there are crazy. I also remember how I was treated when I was in the hospital after the hit and run, and it doesn't set good with me. I have a few cycling friends around my age, but I only see them when they are not working. I know I need to be here with my dad.

Two years ago, Dad had two strokes. Luckily, they didn't do any significant damage, but I know things might have been different. It was good that I was there with him that day. Now I help to remind him to take his medicine and to cook for him. It is hard on me here because I don't have much support in the way of friends, family, and teammates. Back in Waskish, Minnesota, I have all that.

When that time comes that Dad won't be able to travel to Texas or when he reunites with Mom, I plan on selling the mobile home but will continue to make trips to Weslaco to visit friends. I can always stay in a hotel for a few days.

When that time comes, I plan to make my permanent home in Waskish, back home in Minnesota, for as long as possible. I will have to hire some help to mow the lawn or help clean the house, or shovel snow. I plan to keep on fishing and hunting. I grew up doing that and don't ever want to quit. I don't do it for trophies but to put meat in my freezer.

I want to find a church to call home. I've always believed in God and that He made me for a reason. He allowed me to be born with Apert, and He knew that my parents would give me a normal life. He gifted me with stubbornness and determination to chase my dreams. He connected me with friends when I needed them, and He knew I would develop into a fierce competitive cyclist.

I'd like to find a church someday that would have some kindhearted single ladies around my age attending. I never had a girlfriend. When I was young and in school, I felt that my peers did not accept me; then, I had to focus on my studies in college. Plus, I decided early in life that I would not drink, so I don't go to bars at night. Therefore, I am hoping to find a nice woman in the church. I just want someone to go with me to races, go on trips, and see other parts of the United States that I haven't seen before.

Now back to my cycling goals. I would like to set a world record in a cycling time trial on a certified course. I would also like to try and set an hour record on the Velodrome. If I can do that before I am 92 years old, I will. Then I'd like to do it again when I hit the age of 105.

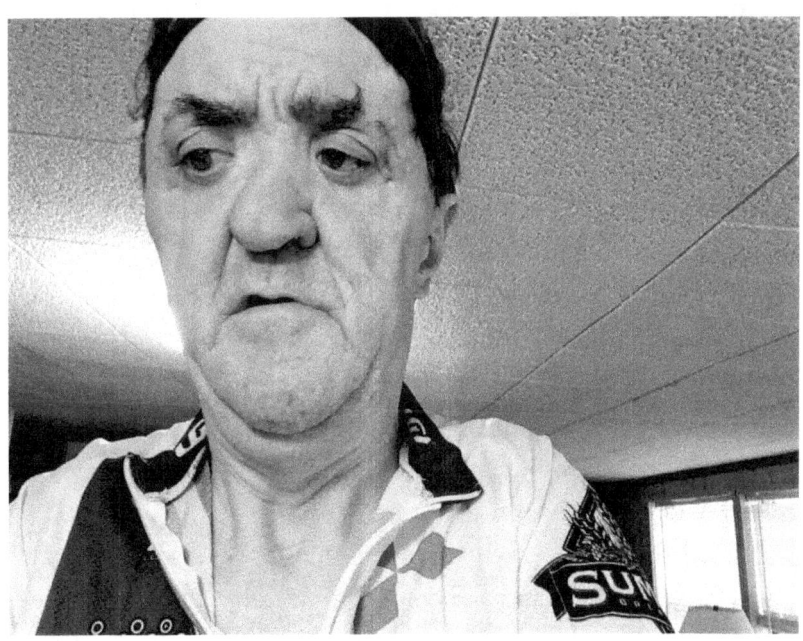

21

Epilogue

Being born with Apert Syndrome has been challenging throughout the years. Some years had more bad days than good days. With arthritis in some of my joints, especially in my artificial shoulders, and my left piriformis acting up more, some days can be extremely difficult. Some of this pain is because I've been stuck inside more with this Covid-19 pandemic going on in the world.

Lately, my daily pain is at a '30' level. My pain scale starts at ten on the regular doctor's pain scale. I don't ever experience a 'zero' pain level. I am in extreme pain every day, and I don't know what my future holds. Despite all, I believe that having been born with Apert Syndrome has been a blessing.

I feel that I was given this syndrome for a reason. I was also given two amazing parents. Even though they had little support except for family and friends, they did the best they could to provide me with a normal life. There weren't any other kids in our area with this syndrome, so there weren't any support or help groups for them.

My parents always told me that I could never use the word "can't." They never wanted me to hear me say that I couldn't do something. If there was no way I could do something like everyone else, I had to try to find a way to do it 'my' way. I had to adapt. I wasn't to have the world adapt to me. It got so embedded in me that there wasn't anything I couldn't do. If someone told me that I couldn't do something, it just made me more determined to find a way to get it done and prove them wrong.

I had a high school teacher tell the class that whenever he was at a graduation ceremony and saw just a page number by the student's name, it let him know that the student had no goals or dreams. His statement frustrated me because I knew that I would be one of those who just had a page number by my name. But I knew that I had many dreams and goals that I had to achieve yet. I did not know when, but I knew those goals could be reached. I also knew I had to take it one day at a time and do my best daily.

I believed in myself, and his comments just made me more determined to prove him and others wrong. I found out many years later from this teacher that he knew I believed in myself, and he knew I had dreams and goals to reach.

I am also very thankful I was born with Apert Syndrome because I did not get into sports until I was in my teens. When kids get old enough in grade school, they can go out for baseball, basketball, football, hockey, and soccer. It is good because it gets the kids moving and active. But they are taught at an early age that winning is everything. Then they get so discouraged if they make a terrible play, get chewed out by the coach, and get yelled at by other parents in the bleachers. I didn't have to contend with that. When I got into bicycle motocross, then into road cycling, I didn't have that pressure from my parents, coaches, or anybody else. The only one getting on my case and pushing me to do better was myself. My teammates tell me to "go and do your best," which is all I need to concentrate on at that moment. If I have a bad time trial or race, my friends and teammates are always there to cheer me up.

Having Apert has helped me make new friends. It took me a while when I was young to make friends. I think Mikol Nelson was my very first friend in school. My best friend, Brad Larson, is like a brother to me. He only lived one or two driveways down from our house. I became friends with Steve Battalion in middle school. Now my friends are all able-bodied with no disabilities. My friends see me as normal and treat me as an equal.

I met Dave Dahlen in 11th grade. They switched up bus routes, and I ended up on the same bus as him, but our friendship didn't start until I started road cycling after graduating from high school. In 1986, Dave and Gerald Johnson from Bemidji helped me win my first bicycle road race. Dave was also the one who got me on my first cycling team, the Loon State Cyclists. My teammates at Loon State all treated me as an equal as well and were supportive. They voted me "The Most Tenacious Rider" in 1995.

In 1999, I joined my current team, the St. Paul Bicycle Racing Club. My cousin, Jeremy Sartain, was the one that made it possible for me to join. But here again, I am treated with respect and as an equal. They don't see me as a guy with disabilities.

Despite all my injuries, surgeries, and medical setbacks, I have remained focused on achieving my dreams over the years. But I didn't do it alone; my family, friends, and teammates have been there to support and encourage me through everything.

My teammates and cycling friends tell me that I am an inspiration to them, but in fact, they are my inspiration. They are some of the best riders in Minnesota and the country.

One of my newer cycling friends, Daniel Casper, is a first responder and a firefighter in the Twin Cities. He has won the National Time Trial Championships along with the World Championships on the Track Velodrome. Daniel told me that I am an inspiration to him. He doesn't know how I can still train when I endure such unbearable pain or when my back is bad, and I'm having morning dry heaves. I told him that I want to reach my dreams; besides, I know that my teammates are training, and I don't want to be left behind.

I have had adults with Apert or parents with children with Apert tell me that I inspire them. Fulfilling that role and encouraging others is another reason I feel I was given Apert Syndrome. Knowing that my life has inspired others makes it more bearable.

My co-workers and instructors that run the water operator and wastewater operator training courses saw me as an inspiration, too. I see them when I go to get my operator licenses renewed. When I saw one of them at a seminar a couple of years ago, I told him that I was a Senior Olympic Gold, Silver, and Bronze medalist. He got a huge smile on his face and congratulated me.

When I go to these time trials, I try to show others that we are all equal, regardless of whether we are able-bodied or have a physical disability. I endured discrimination many times in my life simply because of my physical disabilities.

Now I would like to believe that things may be better for people with disabilities, but I feel that there is still discrimination out there. But I know that my future competitors better not think that they will beat me easily. If they do, they will find out that I am one fierce competitor, just like many of my past competitors found out. Now some of them are good friends of mine.

I hope you enjoyed reading my book. I want to thank my parents for letting me have a normal life. I would also like to thank my grandparents, Max and Pearl Unger, and my aunts and uncles and their families for their love and support, especially my cousins Stephanie Lundin Kemp and Wendy Lundin Kingbay and their families. They are like sisters to me. My best friend, Brad Larson who got me started into bicycle racing, thank you! He was there during many hard times as well. And thank you to my cousin Jeremy Sartain who was there when I broke my hip and got me through a lot. You are all very dear to me.

Being born with Apert Syndrome has been extremely tough. I had to climb and conquer many mountains in my life. I know that there are many more mountains ahead that will need to be conquered. I know I have a great family who loves and supports me. I also have my friends and teammates. I know that there is no dream that I will not be able to reach if I work towards it and believe in myself, which I do.

www.ingramcontent.com/pod-product-compliance
Lightning Source LLC
Chambersburg PA
CBHW072003290426
44109CB00018B/2117